WHAT'S HAPPENING TO OUR FAMILIES?

IONA COLLEGE

Iona Front Desk

24 OCT 1992   03:55 PM   K36B

Item 1 0001 000 309 290

To   2 9998 000 211 203

Due   21 NOV 1992

301.423

G 647

World revolution and family
patterns (Goode, William Josi)
1963

IONA COLLEGE

Iona Front Desk

24 OCT 1992   03:55 PM   K36B

Item 1 0001 000 733 994

To   2 9998 000 211 203

Due 21 NOV 1992

301.423

D 415

What's happening to our

families (Denton, Wallace)

1963

WHAT'S HAPPENING TO OUR FAMILIES?

by

WALLACE DENTON

THE WESTMINSTER PRESS
Philadelphia

3 0 1.423
D 415

PUBLISHED BY THE WESTMINSTER PRESS ®
PHILADELPHIA 7, PENNSYLVANIA

PRINTED IN THE UNITED STATES OF AMERICA

DEDICATION

FOR THIS BOOK on the family, I acknowledge my indebtedness to a host of teachers at whose feet I have sat, as well as those who have spoken through their writings. Those in the counseling room who have shared their distress and anguish have taught me about the problems of families who live on the jagged edges of life. Their contribution is evident herein, though their identities have been painstakingly concealed.

I am particularly indebted to my first teachers of the family, Fred and Roberta Denton, my parents. As well, I am further indebted to Curtis and Clara Holt for their unique contribution to my own family life, their daughter — my wife. Especially to these parents, I dedicate this book.

W. D.

CONTENTS

8 CONTENTS

PART III

SOME AREAS OF STRENGTH IN THE MODERN FAMILY

PART IV

CONCLUSIONS FOR CHURCH AND FAMILY

INTRODUCTION

" Give . . . thy servant an understanding heart." — I Kings 3:9

ALTHOUGH JESUS did not say it, he might very well have said, " Blessed are they who have understanding hearts, for they shall behold new meanings in the world around them." The family is a part of that world. A family is so close to us, so much a part of us, that we may fail to catch the less obvious aspects of what is transpiring. Those of us who live and work with families need to grasp intellectually what is taking place within our families and in those around us; but we must also get beyond this to another dimension, to understand with the heart, to catch the subtler meanings of behavior. This book hopes to capture some of both dimensions.

One of the interesting facets of the nationwide study on the family conducted by Wynn and Fairchild and reported on in their book *Families in the Church* was that one of the most frequently expressed needs of pastors was for greater knowledge of counseling and family dynamics. This is not surprising. Those who have occasion to address pastors' conferences on topics related to the family are usually besieged with such questions as, " What can I do? " and " What does this mean? " Pastors dwell in no ivory towers. They live on the front lines of life. In many instances they may not understand what is taking place or may not know what course of action to take. But they do want to learn! Pastors are increasingly interested in understanding the inner dimensions of the people to whom they minister. They want to know how to bring to bear most effectively the Christian message upon the more urgent facets of the lives of their parishioners.

It is to the task of helping to make the pastor's ministry to families more relevant that this book is basically addressed. It will attempt to do this by helping him to understand some of the inner and outer dimensions of family life in mid-twentieth-century America. It is the inner dimension, particularly, that is difficult to grasp and yet so important. For it is our inner emotional reaction to what we perceive outside us that determines much of our behavior. For instance, a wife who within herself is not sure that she has the kind of appeal that can hold her husband's affection will perceive a real threat in his casual glance at another woman and so respond with jealousy.

Being deep and personal, these inner reactions stir up emotions that may cause the pastor to be uncomfortable and make him flee to the safe haven of theological terms or psychological categories rather than really communicate — commune — with another person. Such was the experience of one pastor looking back on his early years in the ministry. He remembers often being made uncomfortable, during pastoral visits in homes, when he was confronted by the raw grief of human bereavement or the tearing forces of family conflicts. He was unable to understand or to relate to these people in their distress, and his own inner discomfort, partly created by not knowing what to do, caused him to turn to some cliché like, " This is an expression of insecurity," or " Let's pray about it." He would then beat a hasty retreat. Now he remembers feeling inside that it was good to be away from the situation. It is easy for terminologies, for analyses, for procedures to thwart understanding. But they are less painful!

The outer dimension considered in this book is concerned with some of the larger concepts of the family. One cannot understand the contemporary family without dealing with the complex, revolutionary forces of industry and technology that are at work on family life. The first section of the book is designed to provide this background material. The remaining sections will view the family against this backdrop.

It is true that change produces its load of problems, especially change as rapid as that experienced in the past century or so, and more particularly since the turn of this century. The second section is concerned with some of the attendant problems involved in this change. But is all change necessarily to be decried? Much is heard about the weakness of today's family. Does it also possess areas of strength? We believe it does, and it is in answer to the questions just posed that the third selection of the book is addressed.

The approach to the family in this book is basically sociopsychological. The psychological needs of family members are studied within their social context. In the concluding section, an attempt is then made to relate some of these needs to religion and the church. These pages do not contain a theological interpretation of the family, but it is hoped that they have some significant theological implications. Also, the church is involved in an educational program that consumes several hours each week. Perhaps this book will suggest some ideas toward making the ministry of religious education to families more meaningful.

Readers frequently ask, "From what vantage point does this author view his subject?" In a day when "credentials" are important, writers usually expect such questions, and readers have a right to know. This book is, first of all, written from the point of view of a Christian minister who is attempting to understand the spiritual meaning and implications in the joys, sorrows, changes, and conflicts of modern family life. A part of this spiritual dimension is simply "caring." This is the type of caring that cares enough to undergo the necessary discipline to attempt to get a little nearer to the real thirsting and hungering of human need. This is pastoral.

Secondly, it is written from the point of view of a student

who has made an understanding of the family a matter of academic pursuit in his graduate work. In the third place, it is written from the vantage point of a clinician who spends six days a week in a counseling center working with people on the front lines of family conflicts. But since these people are obviously involved with severe problems, and so might be considered atypical, there is also behind this book the experience of working with other families in regular discussion groups during the past four years, for the Family Life Department of the Kansas City (Missouri) Public Schools. One would hope that these more "normal" family relationships would provide occasion for refocusing clinical attitudes toward the family situation where necessary.

It might also be asked through what process the author determined and selected the emerging problems, as well as the strengths, of the modern family with which this book deals. The basic field of personal knowledge on which this section of the book rests is from the aforementioned role as a clinician, of working with live situations. Material was not collected as research in the sense that certain specific information was being sought. However, it is difficult for one to have worked and counseled with more than two thousand people without developing a habit of "research awareness." That is, the carefully collected, personal counseling records of those who have turned for help to the Midwest Christian Counseling Center in Kansas City soon begin to speak out on their own accord as research data. Certain areas of satisfaction and conflict begin to recur with regularity. These areas were then correlated with research by other family specialists. What is said herein is probably most applicable to the Protestant, urban, middle-class family.

PART I

WHAT'S HAPPENING TO OUR FAMILIES?

PART I

STATES OF PERFECTION IN OUR STUDIES

1

OUR CHANGING FAMILIES

THE SUREST THING about tomorrow is that it will be different from today. And the surest thing about tomorrow's family is that it will be different from ours. This is fortunate. Nothing could be more insipid than a changeless world. But our world *is* changing. Old institutions are crumbling as new ones rise out of their ruins; empires are falling while new ones are being born. With each new discovery, our horizons are broadened, and each new technological advance opens the door for others with such rapidity that man's technological skills are outstripping his sociological capabilities to cope with them. This is a part of our problem.

Except for the ocean, there are few unexplored regions remaining on earth. Man is now turning his face toward the vast and seemingly limitless universe above him. But the most challenging frontier that confronts behavioral scientists is that of the human mind. The body of knowledge remaining to be discovered about the mind exceeds what we already know. Of course, as man's knowledge about all fields increases, his potential to use it diabolically also increases. The shadow of "the bomb" hangs over us all. And our knowledge of the dynamics of human behavior increases the possibility of this knowledge being used against us by brainwashing techniques. In spite of these and other fearsome possibilities, these are stirring times in which to live. The challenges confronting this generation are as pregnant with meaning, hope, and adventure as they are with awe and fear.

In a world of change it is inevitable that the family will also change. Modern parenthood is not what it was a relatively few years ago. In our lifetime, family living has experienced radical alterations. This is reflected in the statement made or felt by most parents, " Now, when I was a kid, we . . ." Since the turn of the century we have shifted from an agricultural, rural, and authoritarian society to an industrial, urban, and democratic one. Furthermore, it has been asserted that perhaps we are now white-collared, suburban, and leisured. Those who began life on a farm or in a small, uncomplicated village, and who now find themselves in a highly complex, impersonal, industrial, metropolitan area, quite frequently have difficulty " shifting gears " in order to meet the demands of a new way of life. Many never learn to be completely at home in this new environment, nor do they find comfort in attempting to return to their old ways and places of living. Thomas Wolfe's *You Can't Go Home Again* aptly describes their quandary.

The difficulties involved in radically transplanting people are graphically demonstrated in the experience of a pastoral visit in the home of a parishioner. Word reached the pastor that a church member was unhappy over a matter pertaining to a building that the church was constructing. The pastor decided to make a home visit and found the member, who seldom came to church anyway, rather distant. He excused himself for not inviting the pastor in on the basis that he was painting a room. The pastor talked a few moments and indicated that he too had recently painted one of the rooms in the parsonage. The pastor's interest apparently prompted the man to invite him in, and as the two talked, he poured out his disappointment with the church. It was not like Shady Grove Church in the village in which he had grown up. The church here was so large, the people seemed aloof, the hymns were different, and he rebelled at pledging a certain amount of money to the church each year.

Having vented these feelings and finding them accepted by the pastor, the man moved into a deeper and more personal area of concern, revealing that his wife had been having deep depressions for the past few years and was under a psychiatrist's care. In all of this he felt rather alone, abandoned, and hopeless. People from the church seemed disinterested. His wife's main contact with the church had been an occasional card signed by the members of the ladies' organization. But, as the wife noted: " These are women whom I don't know. They have names but no faces." The man moved to even deeper depths of communion with the listening pastor and expressed his own fear of dying in this forsaken place. He hesitated and then said: " I'm afraid there would be no one to come to my funeral. Who would care? " At the conclusion of this " simple " pastoral visit, the man invited the pastor back. The pastor left, having been once again reminded that it is easy to get lost in this changing, shifting world. The experience of this church member is duplicated a thousandfold in our modern society.

The Lure of the Past

It is this feeling of being lost, or the threat of getting lost, of losing one's bearings, which causes some to cry out for the " good old days." Although they were not always so " good," at least one could better predict the future, and this may seem good. Change is attended by uncertainty and insecurity. Out of such conditions, the past, with its seeming security, develops a glow of appeal. The lure of the past is reflected in the frequent appeals to something on the basis of it being " old-fashioned." The " old-fashioned gospel," " old-fashioned cooking," and " old-fashioned loving " are presented as being better simply because they are from an earlier day. Perhaps the present mania over antiques that causes a person to pay several times the original price of an item reflects an attempt to recapture the security of the past.

To be sure, the past has some valid claims. There is much of the past that needs to be preserved or recaptured. The prophet Jeremiah admonished the people to "ask for the old paths" (Jer. 6:16). A reading of the New Testament reveals that Jesus recognized the value of the past and asserted that he had not come to destroy the law, but to fulfill it (Matt. 5:17). At the same time, he was aware that past ways of thinking and former modes of behavior were not sufficient to the present, all of which led to charges of blasphemy against him. So must we recognize the values worth conserving from the past. This book hopes to uncover some of them.

CHANGE AS A NECESSITY

Though change may be a threat to a few and though some aspects of the past need to be preserved, certain alterations must be made. An organism that fails to adapt to a changing environment soon becomes extinct. This is why dinosaurs no longer inhabit the earth. They could not adapt. And it is no longer enough to cry out for the securities of our quiet past. If families are to survive, they must adapt themselves to a new social milieu. The old woman who, upon hearing the grandfather clock in the hall strike thirteen, awakened her sleeping husband to say in great alarm, "Wake up, Pa, it's later than it's ever been before," may typify many. It is next to impossible for some to grasp the reality that time moves on, and that there is no going back! However, others find new meaning in the words of Abraham Lincoln: "The dogmas of the quiet past are inadequate to the stormy present. The occasion is piled high with difficulty, and we must arise with the occasion."

The Israelites under the leadership of Moses left the slavery and security of Egypt to experience freedom in another land. But their freedom included hardships in a strange land, and insecurity and uncertainty of the future. In the face of this, some longed for the security of the familiar hardships of Egypt, including slavery. Of course, there could be no turning back. Nor can there be a turning back for the modern family.

2

INDUSTRIAL PROGRESS AND FAMILY CHANGE

PATTERNS OF LIVING have changed more in the past two hundred and fifty years than in the preceding two thousand. By "pattern of living" we mean the modes of transportation, methods of communication, types of family relationships, productive methods, and the like. In fact, it is no novelty that many now living can remember well when the basic method of transportation was by horse — a method employed for countless previous centuries. Thus, in a matter of fifty or sixty years we have made obsolete a mode of travel that had stood ever since man captured the first wild horse. How can one account for such rapid, radical changes? Practically all these innovations can be traced back to the middle of the eighteenth century and the onset of the industrial revolution. In fact, it is doubtful that one can fully understand what is happening to the contemporary family apart from a basic grasp of the impact of the industrial revolution not only on the family but on every other human institution, including the church.

Prior to the industrial revolution, people lived much as their predecessors had lived for centuries. The primary modes of travel by horse, carriage, and boat were much the same as their fathers had used generations before. Farmers tilled the soil, using animals to pull crude plows similar to those in Biblical times. The production of goods for family needs centered in the home, and women spun and wove cloth on spinning wheels and looms not unlike those which their great-great-grandmothers and their great-great-grandmothers beyond that had used. The pattern of family life was patriarchal. The hierarchy of family values placed the wife and children beneath the husband, and the church and community supported this concept. It had always been thus and seemed right. When men's hate and greed overtook them, they went to war, using weapons much like those which soldiers had employed when the triumphant Roman legions of Titus swept into Jerusalem in the first century A.D. When men wanted to communicate with one another from a distance, they did so with handwritten messages or by word of mouth, just as the prophets of old had done.

With the onset of the industrial revolution, all these things began to change. Although the term " revolution " suggests a dramatic sudden change, this revolution was characterized by a gradual change during which time all the above patterns of living slowly gave way to an ever-changing variety of patterns. The machine is synonymous with industrial revolution. Men could now employ machines to do much of the drudgery formerly performed by humans or animals.

The impact of all this on the family was rather immediate. One of the first products to be industrialized was textiles. With a series of inventions in the eighteenth century, including the flying shuttle and the spinning jenny, the production of cloth began to move out of the home into factories. This began — remember, it was not an overnight change — to relieve women of one aspect of their roles, that of making cloth. This work must have consumed countless hours of their time. There was a new demand for laborers in factories, which began to come into existence. Thus families began to move into the cities from the farms. As the industrialization of society continued, other productive functions of the homes changed, giving women more and more relief from former responsibilities. Men's work was changing too, as they moved into the cities where they worked in factories or began to travel away from home in response to the demands of industry that supplies be brought from various parts of the world.

Since machines ordinarily do not require as much muscle power to operate, it was now possible for women to perform some tasks formerly done only by men because of the sheer physical strength required. Thus, some women began to work outside the home. Of course, this, along with other changes around them, made them less dependent upon men. Slowly, but surely, the patriarchal family began to wither. As industrialization has continued to permeate every facet of our existence, former patterns of husband-wife relationships have changed so that now women are doing what men formerly did and men are doing what women formerly did. Confusion is rampant! No one is quite sure today what it means to be a man or woman. And it all had its genesis in the industrial revolution and the various accompanying scientific discoveries. Without these, the changes could not have taken place.

However, it must be noted that such changes are not simple and uncomplicated. As Ogburn and Nimkoff emphasize, it is seldom that one comes upon a single cause of a sociological phenomenon.[1] Cause becomes effect and effect becomes cause. All the changes mentioned above have been contingent upon other changes taking place in the environment. Thus, the high rate of divorce in our country cannot be attributed simply to the increased freedom of women. Other interacting factors must be taken into account, such as the changing religious, moral, educational, legal, business, and technological factors. These same writers also note that certain ideological forces are producing changes that cannot be traced to technological or scientific discoveries.[2] But most of these changes can generally be traced back to technology and the rise of what might be called " the machine age."

The specific changes in family life in an industrialized America are too numerous to enumerate. Several years ago, Ogburn and Nimkoff sent a letter to eighteen of the leading

students of families in the United States asking them to list
" ten outstanding changes in the family in recent times." The
five most frequent areas of change in the responses were:
(1) increasing divorce rate; (2) wider diffusion of birth control and/or decline in family size; (3) decline in authority of
husbands and fathers; (4) increase in sexual intercourse apart
from marriage; (5) increase in number of wives working for
pay.[3]

If these comprise the more significant changes in modern
American life, perhaps it might be helpful to discuss them as
a part of the background of this book.

GROWING DIVORCE RATE

One of the most apparent family changes in recent decades
is the increasing divorce rate. Although precise statistics from
earlier years are not available, it is known that there has been
a steady increase of divorces in our country, reaching its apex
in 1946 when there were 17.9 divorces per 1,000 married
females. Of course, 1946 marked one of the first years after
World War II, when many hastily contracted marriages during
the war years were breaking up. Since then there has been a
decline in the divorce rate even though in 1959 there were still
9.3 divorces per 1,000 female population. Or stated in different
terms, in 1946 there were 4.3 divorces per 1,000 population and
in 1962 this had declined to 2.2.

A minister friend tells of a feeling of shock upon hearing
his six-year-old son announce: " When I'm grown, I'll get
married. Then I'll get divorced. Then I'll get married. I'll
probably do this three or four times." The father asked the
son what he planned to do with his children if he had any,
explaining that when people divorce, families must be sep-
arated. The son accepted this fact with surprise and replied:
" You mean if you and mother were to divorce I couldn't live
with both of you? Well, that settles it. I'll just not get divorced! " Probably the 300,000 children who are the yearly
by-products of divorced parents wish the problem was this
simple. Judge Alexander speaks of the complexity of divorce

in this way: " Everybody believes divorces break up families. This is not so. The broken family is not the result of divorce. Divorce is the *result* of the broken family." [4]

Although all marriage ceremonies require the parties to pledge " Till death do us part," the fact that so many divorces do occur suggests that many couples do not take this seriously. Probably what they are really pledging is " Until our happiness doth cease," for American marriages seem to be based less upon loyalty and devotion to the marriage vows and religious prohibitions against divorce than upon the continued ability of the mate to create within the other a feeling of contentment and happiness.

Probably most young couples approaching the marriage altar (ministers continue to perform most marriages) do so with the thought that this is to be a lifetime contract. But when unhappiness occurs later, they have fewer community sanctions against divorce to face than they once would have had. Divorce is still a symbol of defeat in the minds of many, but it does not carry the sting of guilt, embarrassment, and community scorn that it once did.

All this underlines another outstanding feature with respect to the increasing divorce rate — the changed attitude about divorce. The sense of being ostracized, the burn of its stigma, was once intense and painful. An increasing number of people sanction divorce in cases of unhappiness. Probably this change of attitude is nowhere more graphic than as manifested among ministers, who were once rather solidly against divorce on almost any grounds except adultery, in which case the " offended " partner felt almost constrained to get a divorce. My impression in talking with ministers is that most of them personally sanction divorce in cases of extreme incompatibility and unhappiness.

BIRTH CONTROL PRACTICES AND FAMILY SIZE

From earliest times the ancients utilized certain birth control methods. Indeed, Roland Bainton notes that it was the attempt on the part of certain Roman women to practice birth control so as to avoid pregnancy entirely that led to the whole controversy over birth control in the Christian church.[5] These women of senatorial status, because of the scarcity of marriageable men, married men of lesser status. Children born of such a union would take the status of the father. Rather than have this happen, these wives attempted to have no children at all, not merely to space their children as we understand planned parenthood.

The use of mechanical devices and chemicals as contraceptives began to spread rapidly in the early part of the nineteenth century among city-dwelling middle and upper classes of France.[6] Modern technology has continued to develop more effective and less complicated methods of contraception. Those who see the rapidly expanding population of the world as portending serious future problems think that some type of control of the birthrate is imperative. The problem thus far has been one of devising a method simple and economical enough to be used effectively by the vast masses of uneducated and poverty-stricken peoples of the world.

The impact of contraceptives on family life is viewed by Ogburn and Nimkoff as one of the three most important changes affecting the family with a cluster of inventions surrounding steam and steel, and various scientific discoveries being the other two.[7] Families can now have children when they desire them and in the numbers that they desire. Now that children have no economic value as farmhands, it is all the more important that family size be limited. But lest we appear too crass, a deeper motive in family planning is involved. It is expressed well in the motto of the Planned Parenthood Federation: " Every child a wanted child."

Another aspect of birth control is that, for the first time in history, women have some control over when they will have children. This, of course, is of tremendous significance, since it enables them to participate in the sexual sphere of the marital relationship with the same sense of freedom from a fear of pregnancy as enjoyed by their husbands. And in view of the fact that a significant number of women are working, an unscheduled pregnancy presents many problems. However, it is this same feeling that there is a " choice " in whether to have more children or not that causes many couples to complain of the "unplanned" pregnancy. As one woman said, " It might not be so difficult for me to adjust to this unplanned pregnancy if I hadn't believed so firmly that we would have our children as a matter of choice." So it is that many couples not only have to adjust to the unscheduled pregnancy, but perhaps an even greater adjustment is the sense of failure in their "planned parenthood."

Further change in American life noted by family observers has to do with the decline in the size of the family. In 1790, the approximate size of the average household was 5.79 persons. In 1957, one hundred sixty-seven years later, the average size was 3.34 persons. This was a decline of almost two and one half people in little more than a century and a half. The causes underlying this decline are complex, but they seem to have their roots in the spread of birth control knowledge not only of the mechanical but also of the nonmechanical types: i.e., knowledge of the time of ovulation. Various other factors also play a part, such as economic conditions and the decrease of religious sanctions.[8]

DECLINE OF THE AUTHORITY OF HUSBANDS AND FATHERS

The time is not too far past when every marriage ceremony included a promise to " love, honor, and obey," but only on the part of the wife. The men promised only to " love and honor." Few marriage ceremonies today include the word " obey." This, of course, reflects a change in attitudes about husband-wife relationships. " Obey " probably came into the ceremony out of our forefathers' deep rootage in Biblical thought which admonishes wives to submit to their husbands (Eph. 5:22) and be obedient to them (I Cor. 14:34) .

As American families have moved away from a patriarchal type of family toward a more democratic one, authority to make family decisions and mete out punishment for offenders is vested less and less in the husband. Increasingly, his wife has been able and is expected to participate in activities and have freedom of action formerly ascribed only to men. To some young people, the fact that the United States Constitution did not originally grant women the right to vote seems incredulous. There are few rights that women do not now enjoy along with their husbands, and most husbands seem to accept, if not like, the arrangement. However, it has been noted that this decline in authority sounds worse than it is.[9] That is, as women have gained more rights and as the status of children has improved, men, by comparison, have lost some relative status and have declined in authority. Therefore, the significant thing is not as much what the man has lost as what the woman has gained. It is as the six-year-old daughter of a physician friend said, " My daddy is master of the house but my mother is the chief adviser! "

Increase in Premarital and Extramarital Sexual Relations

Sexual experience outside of marriage is as old as the history of man. However, there are at least three significant changes taking place on the current scene. The first of these is what appears to be an increase of both premarital and extramarital relationships. Although accurate statistics covering this subject very far into the past are not available, the epoch-making studies by Alfred Kinsey seem to suggest that there is an increase of such experiences. A second change has to do with the increasing number of women who engage in premarital and extramarital experiences. Thus, the increased freedom of expression and action for women in other areas also appears to extend to the sexual sphere. A third change noted by some studies is the increasing number of " good " women who engage in such relationships. At the same time, there has been a decrease in the number of prostitutes. The number of engaged couples who engage in premarital sexual relations has also increased in recent decades.

Probably the most conspicuous change to take place in American sexual behavior is the freer, more open attitude about sex. Sex permeates every facet of our society. Sex appeal is capitalized upon to help sell autos, foods, toiletries, and farm equipment. Popular songs hint at it in thinly veiled terms. Movies boldly depict it on the screen.

More healthily, sex is a topic for serious discussion in many homes, classrooms, and churches. The new psychology affirms sex as a basically wholesome emotion and experience. But this new understanding presents new problems. Sexual taboos that once provided rather formidable barriers to "going wrong" are crumbling. No adequate substitute has replaced them. More contacts are permitted between boys and girls in informal settings. One of these is the automobile, which provides a mobile parlor, affording privacy and anonymity. This creates real stress. For although the society has removed the barriers to sexual involvement by allowing the couple intimacy and privacy, it continues to disapprove publicly of premarital sexual experience. But on a private level there appears to be a kind of tacit approval so long as one is not caught. However, there is one obvious level where no such approval exists. The parents of the teen-age girls who come to us for counsel concerning what to do with their unmarried pregnant daughters give little evidence of approval of this dimension of sexual experience. These same parents, who may be much more lax in permitting, and in some instances encouraging, kissing and petting for their subteens and early-teen-age children at the "innocent" stages of dating, are little more emotionally equipped to cope with premature grandchildren than their more sexually prudent parents and grandparents before them.

3

SHIFTING ROLES OF THE FAMILY

INSTITUTIONS and movements come into existence, flourish, and survive because certain needs exist in the society and are met by these institutions, or movements. As the society changes, the institutions, if they are to survive, must adapt themselves to meet new conditions, new needs. Failing to adapt, like dinosaurs, they pass into oblivion.

The family came into being with the dawn of humanity because certain needs existed in that prehistoric time that were met by this early family circle. And the family in every society has adapted itself to meet the specific needs of each particular society. Although families have always made certain adjustments as civilizations rose and fell, and as people migrated to new regions of differing climates, in the wake of the industrial revolution certain functions formerly performed by the family had to make rapid, radical shifts. It is the purpose of this chapter to explore some of these shifts briefly. We will also briefly assess the role and significance that the family plays in our lives.

From the beginning, the family has performed the basic role of the propagation and care of children. A second basic role has been economic, in which family members worked together to meet their needs for food, shelter, clothing, and protection. But there are many other lesser roles played by families. Agreement on the nature of these depends somewhat on the student's particular frame of reference or point of view. In 1927, E. R. Groves, a pioneer in the systematic study of the family, outlined four basic roles: the protection and care of the young, the regulation of sex, the perpetuation of the culture, and the meeting of the needs for intimate contacts.[1] The following year, 1928, William F. Ogburn named six basic functions: the affectional, the economic, the recreational, the religious, the educational, and the protective.[2] In 1934, Nimkoff included most of the basic ones listed in the above two outlines and added the functions of the enlargement of experience, the provision of security, and the control of environment.[3] By 1945, Burgess and Locke noted seven historic functions: economic, protective, educational, religious, recreational, affectional, and cultural.[4] In 1958, Nathan Ackerman proposed six purposes of the family: the provision of food, shelter, and other physical necessities; the provision of social togetherness; the opportunity to evolve a personal identity; the patterning of sexual roles; the training toward integration into social roles; and the cultivation of learning.[5] This chapter on shifting family roles will follow the outline of functions outlined by Burgess and Locke. As will be seen, radical changes have occurred in most of the historic roles of the family, shifting responsibility for these to other agencies outside the home.

THE ECONOMIC ROLE

In agrarian societies, the home is a veritable beehive of activity as family members produce most of the goods necessary for the sustenance of the family. Our rural forefathers produced most of the products that they used within the family. These included meat, vegetables, cloth, candles, leather, soap, milk products, furniture, and many of their farm tools. Curing meat and canning foods were not interesting hobbies to grandma, as they seem to be to some modern urban wives. They were serious business. How well the family lived during the long winter was dependent upon how diligent the housewife

had been during the summer. Cash for products they could
not make, such as saws, nails, and horseshoes, came from
the sale of the two main cash products: cotton and tobacco.
Some farmers sold grain and cattle. But the central point of
emphasis is that the family was basically a self-contained unit.

As industries increasingly moved into the cities, more and
more of the productive functions of the family were transferred to factories and shops in town. As noted earlier, one of
the first of these productive functions to be transferred was the
spinning and weaving of cloth. This trend has continued with
gathering momentum until the present urban home produces
hardly any of the goods it consumes.

Probably this shift in the role of the family is nowhere more
apparent than in the area of food consumption. The modern
wife buys cakes from the delicatessen, or, if she wants to do it
the " hard " way, there are ready-mix cakes in a box. There
are also biscuits in a refrigerated tube, bread from the baker,
creamed potatoes in a box, and frozen vegetables in a bag.
And if she does not want to peel, cut, and fry her French fries,
these are available frozen and need only be heated. Of course,
a fully prepared frozen meal is available to the busy housewife, who can place it in her automatic oven, which will turn
itself on and off at the proper time while she shops, and arrive
home to a cooked chicken dinner "untouched by human
hands." She doesn't even have to wash the dish in her automatic dishwasher; she simply throws the aluminum dish away.

But if this is asking too much, the family can always eat
out. Americans are urged to " eat out more often " by a national organization, and we are doing just that. The noon
meal, particularly, is eaten away from the home. Fewer men
are taking to work lunches that have been prepared at home.
Many of the larger companies now provide cafeterias for their
employees. And expense accounts covering meals are making
many husbands discontented with the relatively plain eating
served at home. In the four decades between 1900 and 1940
the population increased 73 percent, but the number of wait-
ers and waitresses necessary to serve the growing number of

Americans eating out increased 390.4 percent.[6]

Obviously, the family has not ceased to be an economic unit. The *type* of economic unit that it is has shifted. The discussion above simply asserts that it is no longer a productive economic unit. The modern family meets its needs through wages for services performed outside the home with which goods and services at home can be purchased. In instances where the wife is also employed, the economic potential of the family is significantly increased. This also means the family will be consuming more goods and services. And consumption as well as production is an economic function.

THE PROTECTIVE ROLE

Historically, the protection of the home was the responsibility of family and relatives. If the neighbor's cow pushed a fence down and ate the corn, this was a matter settled in one way or another between the two farmers. Either the offended farmer decided to forget about it, restitution was made, or a fistfight ensued. If a satisfactory solution is not reached by the modern farmer, he is more likely to settle it in court. Thus, the protection of his rights is transferred to the court. The frontiersman carried firearms with good reason. The modern husband carrying a pistol is likely to be locked up. A " gentleman " years ago might demand " satisfaction " for an insult to his wife by challenging the other to a duel. Today a lawsuit for slander would ensue.

One of the main functions of the modern city is the protection of its citizens. The police force, fire department, courts, welfare department, and health department are all performing protective functions that were once basically performed by the family.

Of course, protective functions are performed not only by the city but also by the county, state, and Federal governments. The welfare program is one example of these governments working together in one protective function. The larger family system of a generation or two ago, when families of relatives lived close together, provided economic protection.

In case of illness or death, relatives assumed responsibility to take care of the needy family. However, the small, isolated modern family is hardly in a position to do so. Even if it is able to offer help financially, the fact that members of a family are usually scattered breaks family ties and solidarity. Thus, the sense of responsibility for needy relatives is lacking. At the same time, Quarantelli presents an interesting report that suggests that in minor family crises, relatives are still the most immediate prevalent source of help. In major catastrophes such as floods, outside agencies are the commonest source of help.[7]

The whole social-work movement has arisen as a result of various organizations and agencies assuming certain protective functions formerly carried on by the home. Children, women, and the aging have been the particular center of concern for much planning and legislation. Out of this have arisen child-labor laws, old-age financial assistance, unemployment benefits, and other types of social insurance.

The care of older people is a particular problem for the modern family. The rural home of the past was spacious compared to the current urban one. There used to be room for grandma, and since various chores, such as canning, were an ever-present responsibility on the farm, there was usually some type of meaningful activity in which she could engage. The modern home does not have enough significant household responsibilities for the children, much less for grandma. She is likely to feel very much in the way and unwanted. She frequently is. With the coming of company retirement plans and Federal old-age assistance, aging parents can be self-sustaining long after they would have otherwise become dependent on their children.

THE ROLE OF EDUCATION

Schools have a rather long history. However, the modern concept of education in which the school is charged with the responsibility for teaching everything from arithmetic to zoology and French to family life is a relative newcomer. At the time when society was basically an agricultural one, the body of knowledge necessary for daily living was rather simple. The early schools were concerned with teaching reading, writing, and arithmetic. The additional skills considered necessary for making one's contribution in life were usually taught within the family. The idea of going to college to prepare to become a farmer would doubtless have thrown farmers of not too long ago into fits of laughter. Yet this is precisely what many young men do in our day, when farming is big business.

Modern high schools teach the girls home economics and the boys industrial arts in addition to the more traditional academic studies. Of course, some feel this is necessary because mothers no longer teach their daughters the domestic arts and fathers do not teach their sons a trade. Fortunately, modern husbands do not expect their wives to know much about cooking. And fathers do not have the time, interest, or knowledge to prepare their sons for an occupation, nor would most employers want the sons of employees learning how to do accounting, for instance, in their company. The point of all of this, however, is that the child's teachers are no longer the parents, but professional people trained and employed by the parents for this purpose.

Not only does the home no longer teach reading and writing or vocational skills, it is also relegating some of its functions of moral, religious, and character education to other agencies. Among these groups are the Boy Scouts, Girl Scouts, the church, Little League, Boys Club, Y.M.C.A., Y.W.C.A., and summer camps. These are supposed to develop sportsmanship, cooperative spirit, competitive spirit, fair play, honesty, moral fiber, physical development, and the like. However, the home does have some role in all of this. It provides the mother. And, as one mother stated: " You know those forms we are always filling out, where it asks for the mother's occupation? Well, the next time I have to fill one out, I'm going to write ' chauffeur '! " Thus it is the function of the modern mother to transport her children countless miles each month in order to take advantage of these activities.

In the early history of our country, children could learn the three R's with three months' schooling a year. During the remainder of the time, they served useful functions on the farm. The modern child spends nine to ten months a year in school for twelve years, getting his basic education. It takes more time because he has more to learn. With the rise of the kindergarten, some children are now entering school at four and five years of age. In the future, all children will likely enter school at five. But this is not the beginning. Nursery schools are now taking children from two to four or five years of age. Although this usually seems to be a matter of baby-sitting while the mother works, some assert that it supplements the home in the physical and emotional development of the child. I know of one pediatrician who suggests that parents take their child to a nursery school a few hours a week when there are no neighborhood children the age of their child.

Of course, all this is not to say that the home no longer serves an educational function. It is still the most potent force in the life of the child so far as socialization is concerned. And this is an educative process. Also, in many rural homes there continues to be education of the sons and daughters in the affairs of the farm. But in most homes the concept of education, which includes the academic and vocational, is almost entirely relegated to institutions outside the home.

THE RECREATIONAL ROLE

Recreation is a part of all cultures. Its form, of course, varies. Traditionally, recreation has centered in the home. Farm families worked from sunup to sundown and had little time, compared with modern families, to spend at pursuits other than making a living. But they did have times of recreation. This might take the form of games in the parlor, a ball game in the pasture, flying a kite, a taffy pull, or fishing in a nearby stream. There were also certain occasions when families got together to enjoy recreation, such as a barbecue, dance, or community sing.

In a realistic sense, the church also provided a type of recreation in that it afforded people a chance to get together with neighbors for fellowship and exchange of information. It also provided for group singing and worship, which in itself is recreating, in the original meaning of " recreation." The rural church also provided for an annual homecoming in which families would gather from miles around to see one another at least once a year. Some churches also had an annual revival meeting, which afforded an opportunity for people to get together. A highlight in other churches was the annual " dinner on the ground," in which each wife in the community tried to outdo the other in baking cakes and pies, and frying ham and chicken. And all the men vied with one another to see who could eat the most. But it was all good fun and recreation.

Some family recreation continues to take place within the home, but for the most part it has become commercialized and focused outside the home. Among the forms of recreation are movies, the theater, bowling, skating, tennis, golf, and swimming. Recreational lakes by the score have been constructed across the country in recent years, providing boating, fishing, swimming, or simply the joy of a cabin on the lake for millions of urban dwellers. The joy of relaxing puts real strain on the modern family budget. A family can easily spend $2,000 on a boat, motor, and trailer — all of which takes some of the relaxation out of relaxing. Some men feel the need for a sports car, and the cost of this " recreational facility " usually begins around $2,500.

Another aspect of this shift of the recreational role away from the home is seen in the growth of supervised play sponsored by the city. Many large cities now provide rather comprehensive programs of summer recreation by trained personnel. In our crowded cities, where ground is scarce, areas set aside for play have become a necessity.

One of the more hopeful signs in recent years indicating a

reversal of the trend that had been taking place over the past fifty or sixty years is seen in the advent of television. There are definite indications that this is keeping families together at home. However, some feel that though the family is together watching television, there is little interaction between the members — except perhaps shouting to one another to be quiet! There has also been an increase in popularity of games for the family. Devisers of games seem to have racked their brains for different and unique games, and these have been put on the market by the score. The more traditional games such as checkers and dominoes also seem to have experienced a new popularity.

Recreation in a modern family is enjoyed less as a family than was once true. Television, family games, and Sunday afternoon rides by the family are hopeful signs that families may be spending more time together. And it may very well be true that the family that *plays* together stays together, to paraphrase a popular saying.

THE RELIGIOUS ROLE

Religion in American life is something of a paradox. On the one hand, a larger percentage of the population belongs to religious institutions than ever before in the history of the country. On the other hand, there seems to be a consensus among clergymen and behavioral scientists that religion, as a potent force motivating American behavior, is on the decline.

The decline of religion as a significant determinant of behavior is related to, and reflected in, the decline of religion as practiced in the home. Such practices include family attendance at church on Sunday, family prayers, family reading of the Bible, and asking the blessing (or saying grace, as you prefer) at mealtime. The home is increasingly dependent upon the church for the religious education of its children. Of course, this is also another educational function of the home that has been largely transferred to an outside agency. Baffled parents often refer their children with religious questions to the minister. In addition to the regular worship services, the religious education of the children is mediated through the Sunday school, vacation church school, children's choir program, and young people's groups.

Religion as a family experience, of course, is a potent force in many families. Couples that are only tangentially related to the church frequently develop a renewed interest in religion at the birth of their children. There continues to be a feeling in the minds of many that every child should have some religious training, and parents frequently develop a new interest in church by the time their child is old enough to start to Sunday school. Unfortunately, in too many instances, instead of this being a family experience, the parents merely drop the children off at church and return to pick them up later.

It is also unfortunate that the church itself often is responsible for failing to encourage the experience of worship and study as a family experience. In most instances the family is met at the front door, as John Charles Wynn notes, and "split six ways from Sunday," with the children, husband, and wife going their different ways.

Of course, there has been a movement toward secularization in all segments of our society. At one time, religion was a central factor of all facets of life — educationally, politically, and in the arts. The earliest colleges in the country were established in order that the churches might have an educated ministry. Many of these same colleges now have only a handful of ministerial students. Some great universities are now church-related in " name only," as the officials hasten to explain. This decline of the religious influence and corresponding increase of the secular will be discussed in a later chapter.

THE AFFECTIONAL AND CULTURAL ROLE REMAINS IN THE HOME

As noted thus far, significant roles of the family have been largely shifted to agencies outside the family. However, as

Burgess and Locke observe, two highly significant and pivotal roles continue to be played by the family: the affectional and cultural. They phrase it in this manner:

In spite of the loss of the historical functions of the family — economic, protective, educational, recreational and religious — it is necessary to realize that the family still retains two intrinsic functions. While various forces are shearing from the family its institutional significance, it still maintains its affectional and cultural activities. More and more the American family is becoming a union of husband and wife, parents and children, based on the sentiment of love, common interests, and companionship. Child development is affected by varied and important home activities. Perhaps most significant are the attitudes, behavior, and relationships of the family that may be summed up in the descriptive phrase "home atmosphere." Family affection, of course, is the chief ingredient here, but others of vital import are family events and celebrations, family traditions and memories, common interests and activities, and informal methods of family control.[8]

Thus far, there is little indication in our society that the affectional needs of the child will be transferred outside the family. However, this has been done to some degree in the *kibbutzim* of modern Israel, where children from infancy are cared for almost entirely by women whose main responsibility is caring for others' children while the mothers work. The parents then spend time relaxing and playing with their children in a relationship that has been described as somewhat akin to that which grandparents have with their grandchildren in our society.[9] Of course, if American mothers in increasing numbers place their children in nursery schools from infants of two years old on up, the nursery school teacher will become a significant source of meeting affectional needs in these children. After all, the children will spend more of their waking hours with the teacher than with the parents.

Probably the meeting of affectional needs by the family is of more importance in urban society than ever before. The reason for this is that modern families are isolated. They are cut off from deep ties in the community in which they grew up, where they knew everyone and were known by everyone, as is still true in small communities away from metropolitan centers. Urban dwellers have many acquaintances whom they call friends, but overnight one does not grow a friend who can provide deep support in the joys and sorrows of life. Consequently, the contemporary family is thrown more and more upon one another for the meeting of these affectional needs. And in those families where the quality of relationships between the members is reasonably healthy, being characterized by respect, warmth, and responsibility, the modern family does a pretty good job of preparing its members for life in a complex society.

In addition to meeting affectional needs, the family is also the primary cultural agent. This refers to what is also called "socialization," or the process whereby a person learns to behave according to the patterns of society. There seems to be no threat to this function of the family, although the community now, as in the past, exercises a profound influence in this area. That American children eat with spoon and fork instead of their hands is a result of this cultural or socialization process. Basic to this cultural role is the development of a hierarchy of values. Thus, the American child comes to value eating with a fork over eating with his fingers. The home also inculcates other values relevant to cleanliness, religion, love, education, and trust. It is Ackerman who underlines the inseparable relationship between values and socialization. There can be no values apart from socialization, and no socialization apart from values.[10] Because of particular patterns of values, a person can be distinguished as an American rather than a Russian. Even one's social class is reflected in the values inculcated in the socialization process. And it is the home that primarily transmits such values.

4

THE INFLUENCE OF PROTESTANTISM
ON THE FAMILY

Sixteenth-century Reformers had little interest in the family as such. Rather than making deep excursions into theological understandings of marriage and the family, they were more concerned with correcting religious abuses of their day.[1] Nonetheless, it was inevitable that the main thrust of their concern would also have an impact on family life. This chapter is concerned with some of these influences.

The shape of the modern American family is the result of a confluence of many forces. One of these is Protestantism. Would one be overly optimistic about its influences on the family to say that the Protestant faith of many of the early founders of our country provided a rich seedbed for the gradual development of certain qualities in contemporary American family life? Among these, perhaps, is the democratization of the family and our high valuation on marriage.

Although this chapter concerns itself mainly with certain positive influences of Protestantism on family life, it will also devote attention to aspects that are less desirable. The Socratic injunction " Know thyself " is not new to Protestants. We must know ourselves — including the limitations of our position. The ability for self-criticism is one of the strengths of Protestantism. Indeed, as David Soper aptly notes, Protestantism was born out of self-criticism about traditional modes of think-

ing, and one ceases to be Protestant, in the fullest meaning of
the word, when he begins giving assent to a position simply
because tradition has decreed it.[2]

In dealing with Protestantism and family life, it should be
noted that there is no Protestant theology of the family. In
regard to the family, the Roman Catholic Church has evolved
a rather highly developed, intricate system of beliefs that are
universally shared by Catholics around the world. Protestants
have no such system of beliefs about the family. Though there
is considerable diversity among Protestants, there are points on
which we are agreed that provide a unity in the midst of
diversity. Wynn and Fairchild deal with some of these points
of agreement and begin with what is probably the cornerstone
of Protestantism — the sovereignty of God. But as far as the
family is concerned, they correctly state that there is no
" framework of systematized, consistent beliefs which are in-
tegrally related to the pivotal doctrines of Protestant Christianity." [3]

One of the challenging movements in modern Protestantism
has to do with explorations into new and more profound
understandings of the family. Derrick S. Bailey's *The Mystery
of Love and Marriage* is possibly the most significant book on
marriage by a Protestant theologian of this generation. In it,
he examines the pivotal Biblical concept of " one flesh " and
its meaning as a basis for marriage. Protestants are also addressing themselves to other urgent matters of current family
life such as divorce, birth control, and church-family relations.
Out of such concerns, one can detect an emerging Protestant
theology of the family.

In the meanwhile, there are certain elements in the Protestant tradition that have influenced Protestant family life and
in some instances have helped shape family life as a whole.

First, the Protestant concept of the *priesthood of all believers* is one belief that has relevance for family life. The
Reformers were concerned with this concept as it related to
an individual's ability to approach God through Christ with-

out need for any other intermediary such as a priest or saint.
Luther's insight that man is justified by faith alone is related
to this in that it affirms that man needs to approach God
through Christ with faith alone.

This understanding of man's relationship to God, it seems
to me, bestows a dignity upon mankind, and upon each member of the family. It affirms that each person is competent in
himself through Christ to move toward God. No one can do
this for him. When translated into terms of the family, this
means that, ultimately, each member has the right and responsibility for making his own decisions not only with regard
to his relationship to God but also in other spheres of his life.
This, of course, does not preclude the counsel and guidance of
others. The priesthood of each person also means that he,
under God, has the responsibility for and the right to make
decisions regarding the type of work he shall pursue, whom
he shall marry, and the manner in which he shall worship.
These decisions are to be made responsibly, but no one has
the right to usurp this privilege and dictate to the individual.

Although Luther was a firm believer in freedom of individual conscience, he and the other early Reformers established a movement that Paul Tillich says was as authoritarian
and conformist as the Roman Church it opposed.[4] There was
little room for individualism, as we understand it, in the first
one hundred and fifty years of Protestantism. But the seed had
been sown. With the beginnings of the Pietistic movement and
its emphasis on individual guilt, religious experience, and personal perfection, the seed began to bear fruit. Modern Protestantism now seems to have a more clearly defined theology
of the individual than of the corporate life of the individual.

The Protestant emphasis on the individual has contributed
to the development of the democratic family. At least it is in
harmony with this type of family. (This is not to say that the
democratic family is necessarily more " Christian " than any
other type of family.) The democratic family is possible when
each member is viewed as a real person whose rights to his

own ideas are both expected and accepted, and who, because of his own unique personality, has a contribution to make toward the enriching of family life. Such a view of the individual is inherent in Protestant thought and has provided rich soil for the democratization of the family. This, in spite of the fact that Protestant families have been, and many continue to be, rather patriarchal. The tendency in Protestantism seems to have been toward a growing appreciation for the individual, an attitude that is an outgrowth and elaboration of the doctrine of the priesthood of the believer.

Secondly, Protestantism has *elevated the status of marriage*. Historically, the church has asserted, frequently in the face of opposition, that marriage is good and not evil. Until the Reformation, however, it was rather consistently placed in a subordinate role with reference to virginity or celibacy. Augustine was an early and pivotal thinker who had a profound impact on all subsequent Christian theology, including beliefs about marriage. His own early sensuous and religious experiences doubtless colored many of his later pronouncements upon marriage and sex. Marriage, he asserted, although not evil in itself, is a concession to the weak and a remedy for lust.[5] His whole treatise *Of Holy Virginity* defends the point of view that God views celibacy as more acceptable than marital intercourse. Sex is not evil in itself, he believed, but lust is. However, since sex never occurs apart from lust, every act of intercourse is inevitably accompanied by sin.[6] A more extreme evaluation of marriage by Jerome, a contemporary of Augustine, was that the only good coming out of it is that it produces more virgins.[7]

Luther, Calvin, and other Reformers found such views unrealistic and without Biblical foundation. They were not long in attacking them. Why, they asked, should the unmarried state be more pleasing to God than the married one? Such a view, they felt, had no support from the Bible, particularly in the light of such passages as, " God saw every thing that he had made and, behold, it was very good," and " It is not good that the man should be alone." Luther was led to assert that it is not only the right but also the duty of most people to marry. His subsequent marriage to a former nun, Katharina von Bora, " established the Protestant parsonage." [8] Indeed, it might be said that he established the Protestant home.

One might ask how it was that virginity and celibacy came to occupy an elevated status in the first place. Probably the clearest statement of its evolution is traced by William Graham Cole in his book *Sex in Christianity and Psychoanalysis*. Dr. Cole begins by noting that the Bible takes a naturalistic approach to sex. That is, sex is a natural and normal aspect of human existence, and as such, is to be sought after. Prior to New Testament times, however, through the conquests of Alexander the Great, Greek thought became saturated with Oriental dualism, particularly from Zoroastrianism, and man was dichotomized into body and spirit. The dualist regards the body as a tomb from which the immortal soul must be released. The goal of life is to transcend the sordid demands of the body and achieve liberation through contemplation. Sex is an appetite of the body, and like all such appetites, it is to be rigidly disciplined. Marriage, according to the dualist, is evil not only because it involves sex but also because it produces more souls imprisoned in bodies. Hence, hymns were sung by dualists to virginity and celibacy. This philosophy early contended with Christianity by trying to infiltrate it. Several New Testament books were written to counteract the influence of one of these dualistic philosophies, Gnosticism. This led John to put strong emphasis on " the Word became flesh " (John 1:14) .

Paul's advice, in I Cor., ch. 7, about remaining unmarried, was, Cole believes, not based on the dualistic belief that sex is evil. It was, rather, based on eschatological considerations. That is, Paul believed that the return of Christ was imminent and the work to be done required haste, with no time for the encumbrance of a husband or wife.[9] However, as the church moved more and more away from its Hebrew origins into the

Gentile world dominated by Hellenistic thought, Paul's advice became increasingly interpreted in dualistic terms. Early Christian leaders, such as Augustine, were thoroughly schooled in Greek thought, which inevitably colored their Christian beliefs. Augustine, furthermore, had been a member of the Manichees, a dualistic cult that left its imprint on his thinking. Thus the church in effect unwittingly assumed certain pagan beliefs about the body, sex, and marriage, and "baptized" them into the body of Christian belief.

Against a background such as this, it is understandable that virginity and celibacy should be elevated and revered as being "better and more blessed than to be united in marriage," to use the words of the Council of Trent. But it was also against this background that the Reformers began to attack this traditional mode of thinking. (But even they were not entirely free of dualistic concepts of sex, since Luther thought that one of the results of original sin was lust.[10]) Marriage is an honorable state, they insisted, which has God for its author and patron. Roland Bainton believes that removing the stigma from marriage is one of the chief contributions of the Reformers. It has profoundly affected subsequent family life by placing it among the highest values in the area of interpersonal relations.[11]

This elevation of marriage does not force young people into the decision of choosing the "high" road of virginity, or the "low" road of marriage. Marriage is not a concession to the weak or a remedy for promiscuity, but a high choice having worth in and of itself. There need be no guilt, no regret over having chosen the second best. Moreover, it would seem that this tends to promote a healthier attitude toward sexual intercourse as having worth in and of itself, a kind of self-justifying communication.

A third influence of Protestantism on the family has to do with the *breaking down of the wall between the religious and the secular*. Prior to the Reformation the lines of demarcation between the religious and secular were rather rigid and clear-cut. The religious life spent in the service of the church was the high road reserved for those truly dedicated to Christ. Secular work, although important, occupied a position of secondary importance. The Reformers found no justification for such a division and asserted the essential dignity and religiousness of all honest vocations, whether priest or plowman.

In our time, there is an awakening of interest in the religious dimensions of one's work. This is a healthy interest. Various publications and discussions on campuses are affirming the basic Protestant tenet that all honest work can be a part of one's contribution to the Kingdom of God, when engaged in responsibly under God. This generation is rediscovering the insight gained by our Protestant forefathers that Christ is the Lord of the whole of life and that he can work in and through all facets of life. By this standard no husband or father need feel that his work is any less pleasing to God than the minister's. But it also has another implication for family life. Fairchild and Wynn note that the Protestant Christian is not only to " be the church " in the daily sphere of his work and life, but he is also to be the church in his home.[12] Of course, this reflects the Protestant concept that the church resides in essence in its members, not in the bishops, as in Catholic theology. Thus each Christian represents Christ to his own family as well as to his neighbor. This also reminds us that, strictly speaking, our true vocation (calling) is the Christian way of life that is to be lived in whatever circumstances one finds himself, whether at work or at home.

A fourth influence on the family by Protestantism is that it has *freed marriage and the family from ecclesiastical domination.* The Catholic Church at the time of the Reformation was an extremely powerful organization exercising not only religious influence but also wielding tremendous political power. A part of its control extended to the family. By affirming marriage as a sacrament, the Roman Catholic Church brought marriage and family life squarely under its jurisdiction. Control over marriage is strengthened by the fact that all the sacraments are interrelated.[13] That is, for marriage to be an effectual sacrament, baptism and the Mass are also necessary. However, as Luther and Calvin were quick to note, the whole basis of making marriage one of the sacraments was a mistranslation of Eph. 5:31-32, where *mystērion* is mistakenly rendered in the Latin as *sacramentum*.

It was against this domination of marriage and the family by ecclesiastical law, with its multitudinous prescriptions and proscriptions, that Luther and Calvin protested. Marriage, they asserted, is basically a civil matter, since marriage among non-Christians is as valid as among Christians. However, they both felt that the church could act as the invited guest to pronounce the blessing.[14] Of course, marriage in the United States is a civil matter. The minister acts on behalf of the state through power invested in him by the state. He is the " invited guest " of civil authority. The church may or may not pronounce a further blessing, but that blessing is not necessary for it to be legal.

There are Protestants who feel that marriage has been removed too far from the church. This has led, they feel, to increasingly secular attitudes about marriage and has undermined its solidarity. Possibly this is true, but there are others who feel that marriage and its relationships need to be free and spontaneous, with the couple free to incorporate into their lives those aspects of the church which appear valid to them. The domination of family life by a church that cannot be questioned is not the answer, the Reformers thought. To them, the church, marriage, and the state are all ultimately under God's authority and stand judged by him.

Having viewed certain positive influences of Protestantism upon the family, let us now focus attention on some possible negative influences. The weaknesses of Protestantism are the weaknesses of its virtues, according to Dillenberger and Welch.[15] If this is so, the first " weakness of a virtue " to be discussed is an exaggerated emphasis on the individual. One of the strengths of Protestantism lies in its insistence upon the ultimate right, competence, and responsibility of each individual for his own decisions, whether pertaining to God or man. As noted earlier, Protestantism has a strong theology of the individual. Partly because of this concept, the early settlers of our country were fiercely democratic. This has also undoubtedly made its contribution to the rugged individualism that has characterized much of our history. When carried to its extreme, however, this can result in a kind of irresponsibility in which one fails to recognize the effects of a decision upon the larger community, and in which the larger community may fail to recognize its legitimate responsibility to the groups of individuals within its fellowship. Such has been the case in some areas of Protestant life, and the family is one of these groups within the fellowship of the church that is frequently neglected.

How is this overemphasis on the individual manifested? One expression is the lack of social concern manifested in some circles of Protestantism. These groups seem to view Christianity as a private love affair between man and God, with little sense of responsibility for the type of environment in which the individual lives. Their concern is limited to a rather narrow conception of the Christian life that, judging by actions, begins and ends with conversion. Another expression of this was exemplified by the action taken recently by one large church that has a variety of religious programs for its members. When it was presented with a plan for an expanded program with a family emphasis, it voted the plan down. The general opinion was that this was outside the sphere of the church's responsibility. They might well have said: " We are concerned with getting the individual ' saved.' Beyond that, it is his business."

A subtle and more devastating effect of this individualism is that it may leave the individual Protestant Christian feeling alone, abandoned, at the mercies of a threatening world. That is, an overemphasis on the individual can leave the lone Christian without a sense of belonging to a larger whole, without the undergirding strength derived from being a part of a larger fellowship. He is on his own. There are those who think that this may be one contributing factor to a higher incidence of mental and emotional disturbances among Protestants than Catholics. The Catholic, though he may rarely attend church, usually continues to have deep emotional ties to the church; he has an abiding sense of identity as a Catholic. The church, like a protective mother, hovers over him ready to offer help in rather specific, tangible ways (such as last rites) in an hour of crisis. He is a son of the church, and this has been " grooved " into him since childhood. This can be profoundly stabilizing when the world begins to " come apart at the seams." Of course, Protestants who have understood the true meaning of the church also have this sense of identity and undergirding. But it can be easily lost if too much emphasis is placed on the individual without balancing this against his membership in the larger body of Christ.

A second aspect of the limitations of Protestantism is that the mainstream of Protestantism has become too closely identified with middle-class culture. To be sure, there are Protestant groups working in both the upper and lower classes, but the main thrust of our faith is with the middle class. Churches ministering to the lower classes many times tend to be the newer denominations with less prestige and influence. This was not true of Protestantism at its inception.[16] Among other things, this identification means that many are beyond the reach of its message. When they are reached, middle-class values and ideals of life in general, and of the family in particular, are promulgated. The frequent result is that, rather than aiding them to get the most out of their own family life, conflict is created by the introduction of a foreign pattern of life and set of values.

Some believe the Anglican and Roman Catholic churches have been more successful in spanning class lines in various parts of the world than Protestantism. However, in defense of American Protestantism, Fairchild and Wynn observe that the class structure of Protestantism as a whole closely resembles the class structure of the nation as a whole.[17] What is being said here, though, is that the main Protestant denominations seem to have become overly identified with the middle class. One evidence of this is the tendency of downtown churches to move out into middle-class suburbs when the downtown area has a large number of lower-class people moving in as the area deteriorates. I know of no Catholic church that has done this, though there may be some. One of the encouraging developments now is that these Protestant churches are staying in the downtown area, though they may need financial help from the denomination.

A final limitation to be discussed has to do with a tendency of some segments of Protestantism to become legalistic. This is particularly true of those groups based on a Calvinistic theology in its purer form. One of the weaknesses of Calvinistic ethics, it has been observed, is its tendency to legalism, to a too-precise definition of sin and righteousness.[18] This legalism was brought to these shores by the Puritans, among others. (This is not to disparage the Puritans, who made many positive contributions to our culture.) Their prohibitions against card playing, dancing, and other types of what they called "frivolity" still persist in many quarters. Accordingly, much emphasis is placed upon sins of the flesh, forgetting that Jesus placed primary emphasis on sins of the spirit and the motives of the heart. This legalism often leads to a lack of compassion, to a difficulty in dealing therapeutically with those who stray from the prescribed path of righteousness. A classic example of this inability to approach the wayward with healing is seen in Nathaniel Hawthorne's *The Scarlet Letter*.

What direction religion, politics, and the family would have taken had not the Protestant Reformation occurred, one can only speculate about. But Protestantism is a fact. It has made its contributions to the world. Some of its influences upon the family have been enumerated. Apart from its religious influence, Protestantism's impact upon the family may be its greatest contribution. Roland Bainton, in summarizing the ministry of Martin Luther, pays him this tribute:

The influence of the man on his people was deepest in the home. In fact, the home was the only sphere of life which the Reformation profoundly affected. Economics went the way of capitalism and politics the way of absolutism. But the home took on that quality of affectionate and godly patriarchalism which Luther had set as the pattern in his own household.[19]

PART II

SOME EMERGING PROBLEMS OF THE
MODERN FAMILY

5

DEMASCULINIZED MEN

WHAT IS A MAN? The answer to this question is one of the most pressing of our generation. The truth of the matter is that no one seems quite sure what a man is like in the mid-twentieth century. Sexual roles have blurred. Men are cooking, caring for the children, and doing housework. Women are working outside the home, searching for a part in family decisions, and engaging in business management. Confusion is rampant! Most modern men seem to know more about what men *were* than what they *are*. " The only thoroughly masculine domain not yet invaded by women," said one bitter male, " is growing a mustache! " Perhaps this accounts for the fact that more and more men are sporting mustaches or beards. In fact, it could be that the practice may spread, if men find it increasingly difficult to determine ways of being distinctively masculine. Women have the distinction of being able to have babies, an area no man has yet remotely encroached upon!

One of the commonest problems confronted by persons who do marriage counseling is dealing with men who secretly harbor fears that they are not men. Males are born, but men are made. A husband may be sure he is a male, but highly uncertain as to whether he has acquired those attributes which he considers masculine. This uncertainty opens Pandora's box to a whole host of problems in husband-wife relationships. A simple request to empty the trash by the wife of one of these uncertain men triggered off a wild fight in which he later claimed she was trying to dominate his life. " She acted as if I didn't have enough sense to know when to empty it," he angrily reported a week later. Demasculinized husbands who are attempting to maintain, regain, or prove their masculinity may find themselves, in addition to being resistant to requests from the wife, involved in what they perceive of as masculine activities such as drinking, gambling, extramarital affairs, and making unilateral family decisions.

Without going into a complicated psychological explanation as to why a man may be demasculinized, it might be helpful to note that certain conditions have developed in the world that contribute to the role confusion of many American males, many of whom are not particularly bothered with feeling unmasculine. Although one can list certain processes of demasculinization, the road to healing this area of human conflict is long and arduous.

What Happened to the Patriarchal Man?

The basic pattern of family relationships in most civilizations has been patriarchal. This, of course, simply means, " Father is boss! " Students of family history are aware of the fact that there have been different degrees of patriarchalism in different societies, and in the same society, at differing times. Probably the extreme expression of male domination was found in the Roman family prior to the Punic Wars. This father legally had complete control over his family economically, religiously, and personally. He could sell his children into slavery or punish them by death if he so chose. Control over the children continued after marriage and included the right to arrange and dissolve marriages.[1] Although the father legally had this life-and-death power, it may be that in actual practice he did not exercise the limits of his power, as is true in the case of many of our own laws. In any case, Zimmerman notes that the Roman father did not have unlimited power if that means that he was not responsible to anyone. He himself operated under certain regulatory forces of the larger clan.[2]

Of course, all this passed, and the patriarchal family as we know it refers to a hierarchy of values in which the husband came first and his wife and children occupied roles of lesser status. The final decision in family matters was the husband's prerogative and responsibility. This, of course, did not preclude consultation with his wife. In a patriarchal society the women stayed close at home, tending to the children and household responsibilities. The men dealt with matters in the larger world. This was a happy arrangement, for this was the only type of family life, they, or anyone else they knew, had ever known. To them, that was the way it *should* be. Good husbands then would probably be good ones today. And tyrannical husbands would probably be tyrannical today, but their wives simply would not put up with it today.

Except for a few pockets of isolated cultures, the patriarchal family in the United States is as about as up to date as buttonhooks. A new family is emerging in its place, characterized by democratic ideals of equality for men and women, husbands and wives. Why did the patriarchal family, which had survived for countless centuries, wither and pass in our day? The answer to this is provided by sociologists who say we are in the midst of a vast, worldwide social upheaval. Probably the only other social phenomenon of equal significance to occur was when men discovered that by cooperative action they could accomplish more and began to group together to form the first cities. The present social upheaval began with the industrial revolution in the eighteenth century. David Mace observes that, in this second change: " Agrarian peoples, their lives deeply rooted in the land, began through scientific knowledge to gain new and vast power to manipulate the natural resources around them. By the use of this new power, they were able to tear up their roots and create for themselves fantastic new living patterns that have led us into the industrial, the scientific, and now the atomic age." [3]

We, of course, continue to be a part of an ever-expanding industrial and scientific era. Scientific discoveries have also changed our ideas about ourselves and the universe. For instance, we know now that men are not by nature superior to women, as Aristotle asserted in his *Politics*. These technological and scientific changes have inevitably touched every human institution from the family to the church. They have uprooted the patriarchal family that had survived countless other changes of wars, rulers, and lesser social upheavals.

Why has the patriarchal family been unable to survive in an industrial age? The answer is that it carried within itself the seeds of its own destruction — its inflexibility. For, as Mace notes, institutions must be flexible and adaptable to constant change in order to survive in an industrial society.[4] The modern family, too, must be flexible if it is to survive. Prior to the onset of industrialism, stability and inflexibility were necessary requisites for survival in a world that itself was relatively stable and inflexible. The patriarchal family continues in our day to be well adapted to certain nonindustrial societies. But it probably has little future in the world as a whole. It is too inflexible. In the space of approximately two hundred years, about one half of the world has moved toward industrialization, and in every society, the patriarchal family has withered to the degree that industry has replaced old methods of production.

Out of the ruins of this old family system, a new type of family is emerging. Some call it democratic, others speak of a companionate family. In either case they are talking of similar traits involving equality and mutual love. But in this new family, men and women are having to rediscover what it means to be a man or woman in a new setting. As a result of the ensuing confusion, many men have become threatened and defensive, which in turn leads to marital discord and unhappiness. Perhaps it might be of help to examine some expressions of this masculine confusion.

SOME EXPRESSIONS OF MASCULINE CONFUSION

A certain degree of confusion attends all new situations. With the passing of time, through evaluation of the situation, and trial and error, the confusion subsides. In our transitional age, not enough time has passed, nor have we had sufficient opportunity to experiment with finding more satisfactory masculine and feminine roles. The modern male knows more about what he does not want to be than what he wants to be. The clearest masculine model available to him is the outmoded patriarchal one in which key qualities were authority and control. But in a society that is emphasizing equality, the relative authority of the male has been diluted. The day of the rugged, hairy-chested, independent man has about passed.

One of the reasons for the current popularity of Western television shows and movies is probably related to the satisfaction both men and women get in reliving our frontier past. The sedate modern American male sits in the security of his large comfortable chair, breathes filtered, air-conditioned air, wears soft, well-pressed trousers, while deodorants block his offensive odors. On his television screen he sees the rugged, swarthy, hairy-chested Western hero whose dusty clothes smell strongly of sweat, and whose fist and bull-like strength are the fear of every man and the admiration of every woman in town. He lives a life of danger, and survives by his wits and his skill with a gun in the freedom of the vast open prairies. In a vicarious way, all this is reassuring to the American husband who turns off his set feeling taller and a bit more rugged. Fortunately, this is enough for most men.

There are those men who are unable to feel sufficiently comfortable within themselves, with reference to their masculinity, to live at ease with themselves and their families. This expresses itself in at least four ways, which will be discussed briefly. Certainly there is much overlapping between these four.

1. *Domineering behavior* characterizes the first of these ex-

pressions of masculine insecurity. These men are trying desper-
ately to prove that they are men by resorting to one of the
qualities of the patriarchal man: authority. The problem is
that these men misunderstand authority and become authoritarian rather than authoritative. They attempt to bolster their
lack of inner security by manipulating those around them.
For strength of personality they substitute strenuous demands.
Ironically, their demanding behavior is more characteristic of
children than of adult men. One of these demanding husbands
perches himself in his comfortable chair to watch television
and then proceeds to find various ways of making the family
wait on him. If he wants a drink, his wife has to bring it to
him, and the children are expected to change channels when
he wants another program. Failure to cater to his needs brings
a tirade about his being the head of the house.

The domineering male is almost always preoccupied with
being "henpecked." Conversation with a male of this type
does not have to proceed very far on almost any topic before
he will bring up the subject. He will express concern about
women becoming too bossy and aggressive. He is also sure that
children no longer have respect for their parents, and so he
will beat it into them.

The domineering husband frequently will have little or
nothing to do with household responsibilities, nor does he feel
comfortable with his wife working outside the home. One such
husband boasted that he had not changed one diaper on any
of their four children.

Mistaking physical strength for strength of character is also
a mark of the domineering husband. One of these husbands
announced to me one day that henceforth he was going to be
the head of his house at all costs. His wife called me the next
morning so angry she could hardly speak. She related that the
previous evening he had become provoked at her and had
forced her across his lap and given her a sound spanking!
Another wife came in with a jagged scar on her forehead with

eight stitches in it where her husband had hit her with his fist when she had challenged one of his decisions. But again, in such cases the uncertain male, in his attempt to act masculine, reacts more like a child than a man. The child in his frustration will strike out at the thwarting stimulus, as do these men.

The demanding demasculinized husband constantly sees threats to his authority around him. He demands to be the " head of the house." He cannot tolerate having his decisions questioned. Though he may seldom go to church, he frequently is well grounded in those passages from the Bible that have to do with wives submitting to their husbands. These he quotes often to bolster his position. In many cases, this same man grew up in a family in which the father was extremely domineering. He is now even more resentful if his own wife and family setting will not permit him " to dish out " a little of what he himself received as a child.

The truth of the matter is that men who are men, and know they are men, have no need to remind their families and *themselves* continuously that they are head of the family.

2. *Sexual problems* may also be an expression of the uncertainty and confusion over masculinity. In fact, this is probably one aspect of the problem in all types of masculine sexual difficulties. However, the roots of psychosexual disorders are complex and deep-seated. There is seldom, if ever, a single cause, but uncertainty is one of the most frequent ones.

Complete or partial impotence can be an expression of the man who is uncertain of his masculinity. He has difficulty with sex partly because he has trouble with his own masculine aggressive strivings. He may harbor hidden hostilities toward women. English notes that although some people may be able to have hate in their souls and at the same time have sexual intercourse, others cannot. They need to feel love in their minds (and lots of it) to energize the sexual organs with pleasure.[5] Even slight disinterest in intercourse on the part of a wife is enough to discourage some men from trying. In other cases, men can perform successfully only if the wife takes the initiative in sex.

Male homosexuals are another expression of this uncertainty. Although the psychodynamics underlying the development of homosexuality are very complex, at least one of the basic aspects of the problem is that the boy in the formative years of his childhood failed to find in his father a person with whom he could identify. The reasons for this failure could be that the father was too threatening and punitive a person for the boy to desire to be like. But the father could also be perceived as a weak, mousy, spineless person whom the boy was unable to accept as a desirable model of masculinity. In either case, the boy was psychologically pushed toward his mother and psychologically became more feminine than masculine.

Two other expressions of masculine uncertainty are exhibitionism and voyeurism. The voyeur, or "the peeping tom," derives a satisfaction out of observing a sexual act. Since intercourse demands aggressive behavior on the part of the male, the voyeur derives a certain vicarious satisfaction out of the experience inasmuch as he has problems with his own aggressive feelings. And the exhibitionist is trying to prove his masculinity by exhibiting himself to women. The greater the reaction from the woman, the more he is reassured within himself that he is indeed a man.

In a rather strange way, sexual athleticism and what might be called the Don Juan complex are sexual disorders engaged in by uncertain men. These are basically attempts to prove their masculinity. The wife of one of these men reports that her husband demands intercourse three and four times every night. Of course, this is not a biological drive, but a psychological one. Each time this man has intercourse with his wife, or the Don Juan with some woman, he is reassurred once again of his masculinity. But there is no end to his search. He needs the constant reassurance of many conquests. Tashman has this to say of the Casanova — another expression of the Don Juan:

The man who still wishes for what he experienced in his earliest childhood, when his mother looked at him as if he were the very center of the universe, may develop a yearning that will forever drive him to try to secure an illusory substitute for that original ecstasy. Such a man has to keep searching, finding and then getting rid of what he has, to go on searching once again. The woman who becomes the wife of such a fervent seeker is getting into a relationship that will bring her more pain and disillusionment than is bearable in a lifetime.[6]

The final type of sexual problem is presented here in the manner of a tentative passing observation. However, my own clinical experience seems to indicate that many of the men with high drives for achievement and success, the type who spend day and night at the office and who may actually " get on top," are the men whose wives often complain that their husbands are sexually disinterested. Doubtless others have observed this phenomenon. But it appears that these men are either bleeding off their energies, sublimating them in the work, or else their absorption in work is a way of avoiding relating sexually to their wives. Frequently this intense drive to succeed widens the gap in a man's relationship with his wife — especially if she herself is not particularly interested in participating wholeheartedly in his achievements. Much of his sense of manhood centers in his accomplishments, and if his wife does not grow significantly in her ability to relate to him in his vocational growth, sexual problems may ensue. His work may indeed become his mistress!

3. *Passive dependency* can also be an expression of masculine uncertainty. Though this man may overtly appear very masculine, a closer look beneath his excessive drinking, or whatever method he uses to reassure himself, reveals a man who is passively dependent. This dependency may be too threatening to admit. At heart he is a shy or perhaps demanding little boy who is still clinging to his mother. His wife has now taken the place of his mother. Beneath the facade of such " masculine " behavior as getting drunk is a man who has

trouble standing alone.[7] And the alcoholic frequently marries a woman who is a competent, controlling person, for he needs the kind of security she can offer. He himself has trouble enacting the role of a man and emotionally has fixated at the level of a little boy.

In some instances there is no facade covering the passive dependency. This uncertain male may have trouble making decisions lest he displease his wife. If they get behind on their bills — he frequently has trouble inhibiting his spending — his wife has to deal with the bill collectors, for it takes too much courage for him to face them. This man may have a good work record, or he may be a " job hopper," which throws much of the financial responsibility on the wife. One of these husbands, whose wife had left him after ten months of his unemployment, continued to argue that he could find no type of work whatsoever. But he always had a good prospect who was sure to hire him " tomorrow." At the end of a year, the wife, who had supported him during this time, filed for divorce, throwing him into a panic.

The passive-dependent husband may express the feeling that he outmarried himself when he got his wife. He continues to wonder why she married him, since he is sure she could have had any man she wanted; but he is particularly sure that he has nothing to offer to the marriage that she needs. " I could walk off right now," said one such husband, " and she would never miss a lick. But," he continued, " I don't know what I would do if she left me." As Blood and Wolfe note, the balance of power is shifted to that mate who is contributing the most in meeting the needs of the other mate.[8] In a patriarchal society, the wife needs the husband more than he needs her. In the case of the man just mentioned, the balance of power is obviously shifted to his wife. He needs her. His own family background with a demanding father, whom he could never please, has inculcated in him a feeling of inadequacy, though he has every reason through his vocational success to feel otherwise.

However, one must not assume that any dependence upon one's mate is an expression of immaturity. The emotionally mature person has come to terms with his dependent-independent needs. The big business tycoon who issues orders, calls London and Paris all day, may at home get his dependent needs met by his wife by letting her " baby " him. This can be healthy. In this way both of them can meet their emotional needs — his for being babied and hers for being needed to baby.

4. *Pseudomasculinity* is the final type of masculine uncertainty to be dealt with here. The pseudomasculine man looks and behaves so much according to traditional concepts of masculinity that no one would ever suspect that harbored within are conscious or unconscious fears about being unmasculine. But they are there. This man may be a big, double-jointed football player who looks anything but feminine. He may be a weight lifter, be preoccupied with his physique and the muscles that ripple over his well-developed body. This hairy-chested, but uncertain, man may delight in engaging in dangerous occupations or activities such as auto racing and high structural steel work. In the military service these men may become paratroopers, Rangers, or go into underwater demolition work. Masculine reassurance is derived from each dangerous mission undertaken. (Of course, this is not to say that *every* man who engages in sports or dangerous activities is proving his masculinity.)

The psychological defense mechanism underlying the above behavior is what psychologists call a reaction formation. That is, the overt behavior is a reaction to the opposite extreme of what is felt within. Many types of extremist behavior are a defense against hidden fears. In our example, a man may defend himself from fears of a lack of masculinity by developing a ruggedly masculine mode of life.

One of the interesting clinical observations in my own experience as a counselor is that the men who possess what are usually considered feminine traits do not often seem to be perturbed by them. The men who are most afraid of being henpecked or dominated by their wives are the ones whom no one would ordinarily take as being feminine. Evidently, men who possess feminine gestures and voice qualities have come to terms with themselves and/or have their sense of masculine security rooted in qualities less tangible than overt "masculine" behavior.

Now, after this discussion of the expressions of the masculine confusion of our age, it should be noted again that there is much overlapping of these. Furthermore, one cannot assume simply that because a man is greatly interested in, say, football, he is compensating for some hidden fear of femininity. But if the contemporary American husband seems to be confused and to have trouble in finding a satisfactory role, it is because he has every right to be confused. We live in a confusing era. As noted earlier, confusion goes hand in hand with change. When social changes take place, the roles of men and women may become confused for a time. It has been observed in Madagascar that the only groups where both men and women make pottery is where it has been more recently introduced.[9] With the passing of time, a division of labor seems to take place, and pottery making becomes defined for men or for women. With the passing of time, perhaps the confusion in sexual roles will clear in the United States.

SOME SOURCES OF MASCULINE CONFUSION

Sources of difficulties are sometimes about as elusive as the pot of gold at the end of the rainbow. This is at least true of psychological causes. Yet, though they are elusive, we must still ask questions and search. There are three possible factors contributing to the masculine uncertainty that is afflicting multitudes of American males and in one way or another affecting their marriage and limiting their own ability to achieve a sense of fulfillment.

The first of these is related to much of what has been previously noted thus far in this book — *standards of measuring masculinity and femininity have changed.* We know what a man was in an agrarian, patriarchal society. But we are no longer agrarian or patriarchal. What is a man in an industrialized and democratic society? Women now compete in the business world, are educated, and are as competent in most fields in which they engage as are men. If women engage in work formerly ascribed to men, what is a man? or a woman, for that matter?

One of the major yardsticks for measuring masculinity and femininity lies in the division of labor in a society. In fact, Margaret Mead notes that in some societies men's assurance of their maleness is tied up in their prerogative, or ability, to engage in certain activities that women are not allowed to practice. " Their maleness, in fact," she says, " has to be underwritten by preventing women from entering some field or performing some feat." [10] This blurring of traditional masculine and feminine roles is doubtless partly involved in current masculine uncertainty. It also accounts for part of the reason why some men want the women to " go home where they belong."

The second cause for masculine uncertainty *lies in the whole process of their learning to think of themselves as men.* Of course in this instance, that is a problem of development experienced by all men whether in this generation or in previous ones. But the problem is probably accentuated in our day. Those who are acquainted with the Freudian concept of the Oedipus complex sometimes find it highly fanciful, absurd, and speculative. This is so partly because of a misunderstanding of the son's so-called " sexual " attachment to his mother around the age of five. To those who are skeptical, it makes more sense if only the word " attachment " is used. Nonetheless, I feel that an understanding of this early relationship between mother and son throws some interesting light on the problems confronted by the son in becoming a man.

The person closest to each infant child is the mother. This means that the first person with whom the child identifies is a woman. One of the developmental tasks of a child, whether male or female, is that of differentiating himself from his mother. This task is relatively simple for the girl, since she learns that though she must grow up and be a person in her own right, she will become a person like her mother and will also have children of her own. All she needs to do is to be like the person to whom she is already attached.

However, in the boy this process is quite different and is complicated. His first attachment is to his mother because she is the one who cares for him. But quite early he begins to get the idea that he is different from his mother. He is to grow up and become, not a person like her, the one to whom he is so close, but a man. Thus he must make a complete shift in his sense of identity. Furthermore, as Valerie Goldstein notes, not only is he not a woman, like his mother, but neither is he a man.[11] It will be years before he can perform sexually as a man. His sister can be used sexually at an early age, and therefore must be protected. His sister will become a woman by bodily maturation. But before he becomes a man, he must *prove* it by passing certain tests of skill, accomplishment, strength, or endurance. This whole process places certain anxiety-producing responsibilities on him that his sister does not usually confront. Still, if the boy has a father with whom he can learn to identify, whom he can emulate, he can make the transition. But if there is no father or father substitute in the boy's life, if the father is too harsh and punitive, or if he is a weak, ineffective type of man, the boy, lacking a model of masculinity, will find himself to some degree pushed in the direction of his mother. The degree to which he fails to find a masculine model and is pushed toward his mother, is the measure of the conflict and uncertainty of himself as a man that he is likely to experience in later life.

The son can also be pushed in the direction of his mother by a father who is highly successful. Regardless of how much this boy accomplishes, he may feel he has failed to measure up to what his father has accomplished and wants him to accomplish.

A third possible source of masculine uncertainty *lies in certain biological differences.* That is, boys lack the biological changes and functions that occur in girls and which reinforce their sense of femininity. At this point, I am particularly indebted to Valerie Goldstein for a significant and perceptive essay dealing with masculine and feminine identity as it relates to theological concepts. She notes, as have some other theorists such as Margaret Mead, that:

This early divergence between masculine and feminine sexual development is repeated, reinforced, and elaborated in later stages of the individual's life. For instance, the girl's history as a female will be punctuated and authenticated by a series of definite, natural, and irreversible bodily occurrences: first menstruation, defloration, childbirth, menopause. Each of these events, to be sure, occasions anxiety for the woman and thus might seem to be the female equivalent of the constant anxiety regarding his maleness which besets the man. Yet these physiological events which mark the woman's life have a reassuring aspect, too, for each of them is concrete, unmistakable proof of her femaleness. The boy's history will provide no such dramatic, once-for-all physical signals of his masculinity.[12]

Of course, one of the main signs of a man's masculinity is his ability to perform sexually. This accounts for much of the teen-age premarital sexual involvements. But, as indicated earlier in this chapter, it also accounts for some of the insatiable sexual urges of adult men leading to unrealistic demands on their wives or to extramarital affairs.

Probably the crowning reassurance of femininity to a woman is childbirth. This is something with which she has lived for nine months. She *knows* that she is a mother: she has lived with it and gone through it. The man's part in parenthood is, comparatively speaking, rather remote. And he has no proof that he is a father in the same way that a woman has proof that she is a mother.

A further difference that can give rise to masculine uncertainty is the fact that when a man's wife gives birth this is something that *happens* to her more than something that she *does*.[13] Even in the sex act, her role is passive, though she can be active. But the man must play the active, aggressive role. This is something he *does*. So in a real sense, a man becomes a man not only sexually, but in other ways, by acting, by doing something, by achieving something. He is in a constant process of becoming a man, as Goldstein says, whereas the emphasis in the woman is in *being*.[14] What we have been attempting to say at this point is that a woman can more easily feel secure in her identity, than can a man, because of her close links with nature through menstruation, childbirth, lactation, and menopause.

Out of these three areas comes much of the masculine uncertainty. To be sure, the last two, relating to a boy's learning to make a switch in his identification from the mother to the father, and in his lack of certain biological reassurances of masculinity, have always been operative. The point here is that these problems are aggravated in a modern world. For instance, if a man demonstrates or proves his masculinity by achieving certain accomplishments, it is more difficult for him to have a sense of significant achievement when women all around him are achieving the same goals with equal or better skill.

The truth of the matter is that all men and women must find ways of validating their masculinity or femininity. The demasculinized male is one who has not yet found adequate ways of reinforcing his sense of masculine identity. He therefore resorts to trying to demonstrate his manliness by ineffective means that still leave him unconvinced and so drive him to more and more immature attempts. Of course, this is not the whole story, since the demasculinized male is more unsure of his masculinity to begin with and probably has an exorbitant need for reassurance. The adequate male apparently finds sufficient validation of his manliness in the ordinary pursuits of life in earning a living, in his relationships in the community, and in his relationships within the home to his wife and children.

The Emerging New Man

The emerging new man stands as a shadowy figure in the dust created in the battle of tumbling outmoded standards of masculinity. He takes shape slowly. However, the new man will be better equipped to live healthily and relate in an industrialized world than his predecessors who have tried to be patriarchal men in an atomic age. In the meanwhile, the contemporary American male at times gropes in the darkness. He is caricatured in the popular arts. Examples of him are seen in Blondie, Ozzie and Harriet, Maggie and Jiggs, and in Fibber McGee and Molly. These husbands are usually depicted as well-meaning, harmless but bungling clumsy males whose composed wives, always a jump ahead, smile knowingly on their husbands like benevolent mothers on their growing sons.

The emerging new man has upon him additional responsibilities not experienced by men of previous ages. As Helen M. Hacker observes, the modern husband, in addition to carrying on many of his traditional roles, has had new ones added.[15] As a man, he is expected to possess certain manipulative skills, termed charm and tact, which were once reserved for women. It is no longer enough to impress people with his industry and honesty. He must also seem to be warm and sincere. As a lover, he is responsible for his wife's sexual satisfaction as well as his own. Failing at this, he may assume he is a failure as a man. As a father, he continues to bear most of the legal responsibility for his children, though his authority over them is diluted by his regular absence from home during the day and particularly by extended absence, if his business demands that he travel. Finally, the modern father *has* to succeed as the breadwinner if he is to feel manly, though his success is threatened by competent women in the business world. His responsibility as a breadwinner is further accentuated by the fact that he is made to feel that he is solely responsible for the welfare of his family. Florence Kluckhohn observes that in many societies the husband knows there are brothers, uncles, and cousins upon whom he can call in time of need.[16] The American ideal of rugged masculine independence leaves little room for such reliance on relatives. Success and masculinity are apparently equated in the minds of most people. The preoccupation of the middle-class American male with money is not so much an admiration of money as such, D. W. Brogan reminds us, as it is an admiration of what money symbolizes — success and achievement.[17] In view of all this, perhaps the modern male is to be congratulated that he does as well as he does!

But what is the emerging new husband and father like? As noted, he continues to fulfill certain of his traditional roles. As just noted, he still supports the family. Although his wife may work outside the home, she does so by choice. He has no choice. Little support could be rallied for expecting the wife to contribute to the family income except in special cases of necessity, such as a prolonged illness of the husband. In a study of masculine-feminine identity among a group of schoolchildren, it was found that the children perceived of the role of support of the family as being in the province of the husband.[18] This role as breadwinner is one of the most significant means by which a man validates his masculinity.

Having discussed various facets of the demasculinized male in our society, I am aware of the fact that there are still others that have been neglected. Perhaps this concluding point should be made, however. The crux of the whole problem for men is not, "Am I in charge of my family?" but rather, "Am I in charge of myself?" Personal observation of men in counseling convinces me that when a man feels in charge or in control of himself, and is sure of this, the question as to who is in charge of the family is resolved. His wife can ask that man to mow the yard and he will see this as no challenge to his authority. He is in charge, in charge of himself. In fact, it may well be that in the healthiest families both the husband and wife feel in charge of themselves, and in a sense are also in charge of the family. Albert Ellis has well noted that the husband who complains that his wife is making less of a man of him was already demasculinized, and his wife is only aggravating his problem.[19] The solution to his problem is not to get another wife, but to readjust and grow up in his own self-concept.

What is a man? Having said all that I have in this chapter, I feel that perhaps there is a very subjective and vitally important way in which a man has to discover for himself the answer to this pivotal question. A man may possess the external manifestations of manliness. But Carl Rogers is right when he asserts that inner truths have to be self-discovered.[20] This, perhaps, is one of those truths.

6

UNFULFILLED WOMEN

"I FEEL like a hungry person with only half enough to eat!" These words are the attempt of an intelligent, competent wife to describe the frustrating sense of emptiness in her life. Her day is filled with " busyness " at home, mad dashes across town to various meetings, and yet in it all she feels that something is lacking. Somehow, all her activities at home and in the community leave her with a gnawing sense of incompleteness.

This wife is not alone. Her number is legion. If the American man is suffering from hidden fears of being unmasculine, his feminine counterpart is probably the unfulfilled wife. These are women who simply cannot find a sense of deep and abiding self-fulfillment in the ordinary pursuits of life within the home. They may assume that the problem lies in their marriage and seek a new love. But still something is incomplete. And it is this sense of not finishing something that plagues so many modern women. Their numbers populate the waiting rooms of counselors, psychologists, and psychiatrists, as they try to find answers to their predicament. Some seek answers by becoming busier and busier. For some this is enough. Others continue in their frustration.

All this is a part of the modern woman's predicament — she finds herself being expected to invest her energies in the home, but cannot find this completely fulfilling. But working outside the home presents its problems as well. So she is torn within. It is to this group of women that Anne Morrow Lindbergh's best seller *Gift from the Sea* probably makes its greatest appeal.[1] For Mrs. Lindbergh has captured in an unusually perceptive way the inner strivings of a woman learning to live the various stages of life in a complex world.

One of our major problems in this area is being able to view the current human situation from a feminine vantage point. Too long we have used concepts given to us by men. Even women, themselves used to thinking in terms of masculine concepts and standards, have difficulty providing challenging new ways of understanding the problem. But the contributions of some women to this field are highly impressive. That they can so freely express themselves with significant observations is a reflection of the change taking place in the role of women. Some of the most penetrating insights have come from women such as Margaret Mead, Helene Deutsch, and Florence Kluckhohn. And a provocative article by Valerie Goldstein suggests that perhaps even our theology is overloaded with concepts from a masculine view of the human predicament and needs tempering with insights from a feminine orientation.[2]

THE PLIGHT OF THE MODERN WOMAN

Basically, the difficulties confronted by modern woman are part and parcel of the conflicts experienced by modern man. In the wake of the industrial revolution the roles of both men and women have become confused. Since this has been discussed in previous chapters, it will not be necessary to go into detail again. Suffice it to say that although men may not be quite sure what it is to be a man, neither are women sure what it is to be a woman. In some respects, the industrial revolution hit women harder because it destroyed their traditional means of achieving a sense of purpose and fulfillment. It did this partly by removing from the home its basic productive and economic functions. Consequently, the home is no longer the significant beehive of activity that it once was. And the wife was the " queen bee " of this beehive. Her contribution was indispensable to the family welfare. The modern home is still the center of much activity, but the activity lacks its former importance. This frequently leaves the wife feeling empty. Going to the grocery for a cake hardly leaves one with the sense of fulfillment derived from making one " from scratch." Even if she does bake a cake " from scratch," it does not have the significance of being done out of necessity, as it did for her grandmother.

As factories have taken over more and more functions formerly performed within the home, the prestige of the home, at least as an economic unit, has declined. Our values have shifted so that we now place paramount importance on succeeding and achieving in the world outside the home. The most impressive measure of success is the financial one. The dollar seems such a " right " yardstick for measuring achievement, and even the churches have fallen prey to making the size of their budgets a major measure of success. Obviously, anything that brings in the money is a success. There is almost a tacit agreement that if it is financially rewarding, it is right.

It might be well to note here that although this financial standard of measurement brings certain problems to women who marry, it has helped to clarify the role of their sisters who, for various reasons, are single. Their pursuit of employment and a career at least has its financial rewards. Although deprived of the satisfactions of a family, they can compensate for this through the satisfactions derived from their work. In a realistic sense, the work of many single women becomes their " family." More will be said about this in the section dealing with strengths of the modern family.

Where does all this leave the wife? On the shelf, if she measures her significance by her economic value in the home. Although it would cost hundreds of dollars to hire her services, neither she nor her husband seems to feel that this is too important. No one else does, either. If this statement is doubted, take note of the next woman who is introduced from a platform. Her academic and vocational accomplishments will be lauded and heralded, but not a word about her domestic skills. In fact, it would be a joke to say, "and she is an outstanding housewife." As Paul Morentz observes, no woman has ever yet been awarded an LL.D. for staying home.[3] Thus, as the home has been devaluated in the minds of both men and women, the wife who is left at home is likely to experience a sense of insignificance and unfulfillment. One's self-concept is closely tied to his work. If he is doing insignificant work, he feels insignificant. The converse is true as well. The most pivotal work taking place in any city is not in the office, court-house, city hall, university, or church. It is in the home. For it is primarily the home that nurtures and molds us into the adequate or inadequate people we later become. However, the woman's role in all this remains confused.

Pearl Buck, in *Of Men and Women,* notes that one of the ways women have attempted to cope with their problem is to move out of the home into a man's world. If this is where the significant — economic — activity lies, and our culture says that it does, then many women will have to move into this world if they are to achieve a sense of significance and fulfillment. Although this began before the turn of the century, it is only in more recent decades that large numbers of women have pursued this path. Wars have encouraged this trend. In the years between 1940 and 1952, which include World War II and the Korean War, the number of working married women almost doubled. At the same time, the number of employed women with children more than tripled.[4] At present, approximately one third of the labor force is comprised of women.

At the same time that women have been moving into the labor market, other changes have been taking place in the behavior of American women. Much of this is a trend toward what was formerly considered masculine. Respectable women now smoke, wear slacks, frequent bars, have their own bank accounts, and engage in " masculine " sports. Many own autos, and some even do their own repairs. Others point to the fact that women are engaging in more masculine, or violent, methods of suicide.[5] Robert Coughlan says that some psychiatrists are alarmed by this trend toward the converging of male and female roles. Out of what they call " sexual ambiguity " emerge assertive women, and passive and irresponsible men.[6] As a result, he continues, neither sex can provide or derive the necessary satisfactions out of marriage.

Dr. Kermit Phelps is of the opinion that perhaps the emerging man and woman is " bisexual." That is, they can shift their responses as the situation demands. Thus a woman may be assertive on the job and more passive at home. A man's work may demand little aggressiveness, but at home he can shift to taking the initiative.[7]

CONFLICTING FEMININE VALUES

Our society is not alone in its cultural contradictions, but we have our share. We begin confronting contradictions rather early. The small boy is told he is too *little* to operate the new stereo hi-fi, and when he cries about it, he is told he is too *big* to cry! So life begins to get rather confused. In regard to their roles, women also confront conflicting cultural values, which frustrates their attempt at achieving a sense of personal fulfillment. There is obvious overlapping in the conflicts listed below.

First, they are told that housework is a grind and drudgery, and if they go outside to work, they are told to go back home where they belong. This is particularly true of working mothers who frequently feel guilty anyway about working. Work at home is almost always depicted in popular literature and discussion groups as tedious, monotonous, and wearing on the nerves. Is it any wonder that under these circumstances women have difficulty discovering a sense of achievement in the home? When a mother communicates this feeling to her daughter, as she surely will, it takes no psychological acuity to understand why the daughter becomes a wife who cannot experience a sense of accomplishment at having put in a hard day's work at home.

Secondly, women are told not only to be good mothers, which means staying at home, but also that housework at home is drudgery. Florence Kluckhohn asserts that Americans have a strong sentimental attachment to motherhood and that we place a high value on women being good mothers.[8] This is attested to by mothers' clubs, the wide sale of books on child rearing, and the frequency of trips to pediatricians. Few shortcomings can hurt a woman more than to feel that she has failed as a mother. Failing as a wife is not so disturbing. Though she takes great pride in being a good mother, the American wife apologetically says she is " just a housewife." So, in the conflict, if being a housewife is unfulfilling and being a good mother means staying at home, what is she to do? Furthermore, if she takes pride in being a good mother, she runs the risk of being accused of " momism."

A third conflict lies in educating a girl to use her mind and then, tacitly at least, communicating the feeling that domestic work is unchallenging and demands little intellectual skill. If she is still unconvinced, the fact that the most uneducated lower-class woman can usually find employment doing domestic work for people on the " right side of the tracks " is evidence enough. So what is this wife who has a degree hanging on the wall to do with her education — besides dust the diploma?

A final conflict arises out of a definition of the model mother and wife as being one whose primary concern is the home, children, husband, and certain community projects, but at the same time presenting the outside world as being the more significant sphere in which people make contributions. The modern wife may feel that she is not making a significant contribution to the family, or the world in general, unless she is working outside the home. But the image of the model home-oriented wife may haunt her to a greater or lesser degree.

With these inconsistent and conflicting attitudes and expectations operative, it is little wonder that many American women have difficulty experiencing a sense of personal self-fulfillment within the home.

DEVELOPING NEW APPROACHES TO FULFILLMENT

If one of our society's chief problems is a confused definition of the feminine role, as Florence Kluckhohn asserts, what constructive steps can be taken to clear the confusion? [9] This is the difficult part. Defining social problems always seems easier than providing workable answers. But diagnosis must precede treatment, and a problem must be defined in order for possible solutions to be discovered.

One of the reasons the modern wife has difficulty achieving a sense of fulfillment is that she has no adequate model of what a wife in her situation should be like. As far as the middle-class wife is concerned, there have never been a large number of wives in her situation. What is an intelligent, educated, socially conscious wife, who has been relieved of many responsibilities at home, to do or be? How can a woman who has been trained to enjoy the challenge of ideas achieve a sense of fulfillment in a society that has not yet learned to provide adequate outlets for her interests? Slowly, a model of this new wife and mother is emerging. Nelson Foote believes that a prototype is to be found in the women of the educated and mostly salaried upper middle class.[10] These women are important, not so much because of their numbers, but because they provide models for the public, moving them toward a concept of a wife and mother who is more adequate to meet the needs of a changed society.

Perhaps the suggestions below will provide some guideposts for constructive thinking.

First, there needs to be a reassessment of our attitudes toward work within the home. Margaret Mead says: " Being a real homemaker is a really important thing if a woman does it well. And we're a rich enough society so that we ought to let every mother of children stay at home if she wants." [11] However, our attitude toward the home seems to be succinctly stated in the currently popular phrase "the trapped house-wife." That this idea sums up the feelings of so many Ameri-can wives is attested to by the fact that the largest audience response to a series of television programs dealing with prob-lems of the modern woman was to the one on the trapped housewife. [12]

Though the wife of a few decades ago lived a life rather narrowly circumscribed by the home, it was not without its rewards. Domestic skills were highly valued by the society, and husbands frequently wrote glowing accounts of their wives' diligence and management of the home. Although a man then might have been concerned about his prospective wife's skill in the domestic arts, the modern husband is more likely to be concerned as to whether she has a college education or job training. That is, domestic skills are not so highly valued in contemporary American society. We do value financial skills as represented by the ability to work.

This materialistic trend toward measuring so many values by their economic worth needs to be reevaluated. The laugh of a baby cannot be measured economically. But if a baby laughs and continues to laugh as he grows up, that is due in no small part to the quality of care he has received from his mother. Or we need to reevaluate the attitude pervading so-ciety that causes women to say apologetically, "I'm just a housewife." A well-kept home cannot be measured economi-cally, nor can the contentment of the husband in that home. It seems that more value should be placed on such work, particularly since poor housekeeping is one of the frequent complaints of husbands.

Most complaints that wives make to me about housework being unfulfilling are directed at its monotony and the wear-ing effects of the full-time care of small children. It is an end-less task of cleaning and recleaning, washing and rewashing. By the end of the day, mothers may feel guilty for having

yelled at the children all day to "put this up," and "get out
of that." Of course, as many women discover, their husbands'
work outside the home has its endless routine and its grind
of meaningless activity. But granting that much of the care of
the home is repetitious and distasteful, cannot new avenues
of creativity and expression be discovered?

In 1934, George Belane wrote an article for *Harper's Magazine* in which he asserted, "A home is a perfect environment
for self-expression of every type." [13] Doubtless some women will
wryly observe that the author of that article, as well as the
author of these observations, is a man, and therefore hasten
to discount the suggestions. However, though nearly three
decades have passed since Mr. Belane made his observation,
it would seem that the home still offers the challenge of self-
expression for women who seek it. I remember very well the
excitement of one wife who came into my office one day to
announce that during the week she had baked several loaves
of bread and had been overwhelmed by the enthusiastic response of her husband and children. She had originally sought
help because she was suffering from little more than sheer
boredom and unfulfillment at home. Baking bread made her
feel alive again!

Although a wife cannot build her life around the creativity
of baking a loaf of bread, there are doubtless many opportunities for creativity in the kitchen. The daily diet of most
Americans, Florence Kluckhohn feels, is rather drab and un-
interesting. There must be countless adventures in preparing
and eating new and different foods.[14] (Of course, this has its
hazards, since many women who have the reputation of being
really good cooks seem to also have a problem with over-
weight!) There are adventures in home decoration, money
management, shopping, and child rearing. Many a mother feels
that even a Ph.D. in child psychology would be challenged
by the situations she confronts daily with her children.

One of the first steps in this reevaluation of work within
the home is for wives themselves to work on their attitudes

about being "just housewives." Few people will respect their work if they do not. Like minority groups, they need to stop thinking of themselves as inferior, and learn self-respect.

All this having been said, perhaps cognizance should be taken of the opinion expressed by many urban wives that if they did value their home and take pride in it, who would be there to appreciate it? It is basically a dormitory. Though they spend hours on the meals, the family gulps them down with such haste that "the food hardly touches a tonsil," to quote one wife. Then there is a mad dash off to a ball game, a club meeting, a rehearsal — hardly an encouraging situation to the wife who invests herself in the home.

Ray Baber notes that the wife who focuses on the routine, manual-labor aspects of her role is certain to feel unfulfilled. But if she can see her tasks in the larger perspective of their effects on the whole family and its well-being, she has made an important step toward perceiving of herself as a *homemaker* rather than a housewife.[15]

A second step toward developing new approaches to fulfillment is a reevaluation of our attitudes toward working mothers. Regardless of the reason why some women go to work, there are two million fatherless families in our country and the mothers in these families must go to work. Although there are still pockets of resistance to women working or entering certain occupations, there appears to be pretty widespread acceptance of the fact that women can and do work outside the home. There is not so wide an acceptance of mothers of small children working, even by mothers who work. And there is a special resistance to mothers who work with no apparent need for doing so. One of the chief concerns of working mothers has to do with the effect of their working upon the children. Johnny's poor grades, his fighting with neighborhood children, his introversion, may all be attributed to the warping effects of her spending so much time away from the home.

One of the most important considerations with regard to employed mothers has to do with the type of care provided while the mother is away. David Mace notes that Russian mothers of young children are *expected* to work in factories and offices. Although it is difficult to compare two such widely divergent societies, this apparently has no outstanding ill effects on the Russian children. This is partly so because well-equipped and well-staffed nurseries are provided at the place of employment and the mother is called from her work if it becomes necessary for her to care for her child.[16]

If mothers in our society are to work, perhaps more attention should be devoted to providing adequate mother-substitute care for the children. Presently, mothers are frequently forced to leave their children with women inadequate both educationally and emotionally, or switch them from person to person, destroying the children's sense of continuity or security. Is it too much to expect that, in the future, companies will provide free nursery service in addition to other " fringe benefits "? Beyond this, more high-caliber research is needed on the various problems of employed mothers, including the impact of their employment on their children, their husbands, and themselves.

A third possibility in developing opportunities for fulfillment has to do with finding significant job opportunities for the women who are not interested in full-time employment. This group includes a vast number of women with smaller children as well as those women whose children are grown. These women frequently have difficulty achieving a sense of complete fulfillment doing volunteer work in the P.T.A., church, or collecting funds for some worthy cause. The feverish dash all over town to this and that minor meeting, sometimes simply to plan other meetings, is indicative of how frustrated they are.

An important suggestion by Kluckhohn for this problem has to do with the development of part-time careers and jobs for women.[17] Although " part-time " usually denotes some type of inconsequential work, she feels that with shorter work-

weeks it is possible for business and industry to devise significant work opportunities for these trained and educated women
who lack adequate outlets in significant channels.

In reevaluating our attitudes toward employed women, it
might be well to remember that thus far women have seemed
to make their greatest contributions outside the home in occupations that involve relationships to people. Teaching, nurs-
ing, social work, selling, secretarial work, and medicine are
among these fields. Perhaps women should be encouraged to
consider the occupations in which they are more likely to
achieve a sense of success and personal fulfillment, and room
should be made for their skills in those occupations. Lamar
Empey, in a study of nearly 2,000 high school seniors, found
that 75 percent of the girls preferred occupations that en-
abled them to work with people whereas only 30 percent of
the boys desired such work.[18] Boys usually prefer working
with abstract ideas and the manipulation of objects. In working with people, perhaps a woman is most nearly in harmony
with her traditional role within the home, where her basic
responsibility is the care of the people within that home.

A fourth step toward helping women achieve a sense of
fulfillment lies in learning to live life by chapters. One's role
is seldom, if ever, static. It constantly changes. The role of a
mother with small children is not the same as that of a middle-
aged mother. It is because of this change that many mothers
are discovering that they can both be mothers at home and
be employed outside the home. They do this through what
one mother described as living her life in " chapters." Upon
completing college, she said, she decided to teach. This was
chapter one. Then a handsome young man asked her to
marry him, which she did, and they had a family. That was
chapter two. She stayed home with the children until they
were in school and now she has gone back to teaching, which
begins chapter three. The fourth chapter will begin when
the children are gone from home and she is confronted with

an "empty nest." She feels that she has been able to stay with the children during the most crucial years of their lives and can now go back to teaching without sacrificing her children for her career.

Possibly it is this "chapter" approach to a woman's role to which Nelson Foote referred when he said, "The current trend in both the popular and professional thinking is toward the recurrent reconciliation of plural interests in ways peculiar to each phase of the life history." [19]

All this having been said, there is a fifth step in developing new approaches for fulfillment in women. This is simply the fact that *women need to be free to explore responsibly the avenues of personal fulfillment.* ("Responsibly," because there are obvious limits to all human freedom. The search for fulfillment, like the search for happiness, can become nothing more than self-centered groping at the expense of everyone else in the family. It can also be a means of self-discovery.) Cultural anthropologists observe that there are wide differences in what is considered the feminine role in various societies. Feminine behavior in one society may be masculine in another. What was meaningfully feminine in the mid-nineteenth century may leave women in the mid-twentieth century feeling highly frustrated. Role expectations have changed. Therefore, we must not try to put "Saul's armor on David." It will not fit.

Emil Brunner expresses very well the point here when he asserts: "This is why it is absolutely impossible to put down in black and white, as a universal rule, which spheres of activity 'belong' to woman and which do not. This can only become clear through experience, and for this experience first of all the field must be thrown open." [20] As the field of activity is thrown open, women can find new ways of expressing and elaborating upon their femininity. For some, this may mean directing their full energies into the home. Others may desire additional outlets in the larger world. But each must be free as she endeavors to discover what it means to be feminine in the mid-twentieth century. In so doing, perhaps both men and women can discover that women who choose to express a part of themselves outside the home need not be masculine but can be as thoroughly and excitingly feminine as grandma ever was to grandpa.

7

ANXIOUS PARENTS

" MY SON drew a dirty picture at school," said the distressed, anxious mother who was sitting across from me. " I wonder where I have failed as a mother." The words " I wonder where I have failed " are echoed and reechoed by countless American parents who have lost confidence in themselves and assume that *all* problems confronted by the children are due to some failure on their part as parents. The truth of the matter is that some problems are simply normal developmental stages and that drawing an occasional " dirty " picture is engaged in by most boys. The anxiety of a parent over such situations is likely to create a more serious difficulty than the one they hope to resolve.

The experience of persons who deal with parents in discussion groups, family seminars, and personal counseling is that doubt and anxiety about being adequate parents is one of the central concerns of modern parents. This is particularly true of parents in the middle class. Of course, this generation of parents is not the first to be anxious. Other generations have had their anxieties. Possibly the father of the prodigal son wondered whether he had handled his son wisely. However, our anxiety is more acute, and we certainly rely heavily on various " experts." For most Americans, few values take precedence over being a good parent. The door-to-door salesman is sure to make a sale if he can convince a mother or father that his product will make them better parents. If they are resistant, he may ask accusingly, "Don't you love your children?" Too often that withers sales resistance.

What are these uncertain parents like and why are they so anxious?

ANXIOUS PARENTS IN AN UNCERTAIN WORLD

The uncertainty of parents with regard to their adequacy is partly a reflection of their uncertainty over their roles as men and women. Beyond this, it reflects a general uncertainty created by rapid, turbulent social changes. In previous chapters, it has been observed that the role of husband and wife has undergone radical alterations. So has the role of parents and children. The "house rules" once called for children to be seen and not heard. Few believe that anymore. In democratic homes, they are *expected* to participate in family conversations and decisions. The latter, especially, was an unheard-of matter in patriarchal times.

In keeping with the American ideal of being independent and self-sufficient, parents may try to make decisions on their own about their children. Herein lies a conflict: on the one hand, they feel a need for being independent of outside help with the children, but on the other hand, their lack of self-confidence pulls them toward seeking counsel. Anxious parents may spurn advice on the basis that it is a sign of weakness. This can be highly frustrating. Much of their independence of thought can become a pseudoindependence whose loud proclamations attempt to cover underlying insecurity. If grandparents who have already traveled the road of parenthood, offer guidance, this is scornfully rejected and depreciated as being old-fashioned advice. But, as Nathan Ackerman observes, this rejection of the grandparents backfires, for the "young parents attach to themselves the same doubt and disrespect they project onto the grandparents." [1]

Having rejected the counsel of grandparents, the young

couple may turn to their contemporaries for help. Free advice is an ever-present commodity, but those who are most eager to offer it are frequently just as insecure, and bolster their own uncertainty by giving generous amounts of advice. However, their advice is often rejected because doubtful parents may also doubt other parents. Having exhausted all resources, the couple may seek help from professionals in the community. But this too may be rejected, for the counselor often finds that he is but one in a whole series of counselors whom the couple has consulted.

There are several reasons why parents are anxious. The first, already mentioned, is the confusion arising out of rapid social changes. A second reason why parents are anxious and quick to blame themselves for the problems of their children is that in so doing they create an illusion of being in charge of the situation.[2] This is one type of defense to which insecure people may resort. "I brought it on myself" is their motto. Their line of thought is that if *I* brought it on myself, and external conditions did not, then I must be in charge.

A third element involved in parental self-blame is that family specialists may have overdone the matter of trying to develop responsible parenthood. During the years of World War II and immediately after, there was an effort to get the public to assume more responsibility for children whose parents had been engaged in war, in the war effort, or were now in school on the GI Bill. Perhaps the specialists oversold their idea, so that some people now assume that children are not responsible for *any* of their behavior and that the parents are entirely to blame.

Finally, parental guilt over failures in their children has been aggravated by a philosophy pervading our society that man is ultimately in charge of his fate. Stevenson and Milt observe that our forefathers were at the mercy of the elements in whittling out a life for themselves.[3] They hoped that everything would work out all right. Whether it did or did not was viewed by them to be God's will, or a part of "man's lot." They accepted life's fortunes and misfortunes as being controlled by powers beyond themselves. But in recent decades a philosophy has developed that asserts that man's fate is largely in his own hands. If failure and misfortune arise, he has only himself to blame. The ability to control the physical world in a modern age leads man to assume that if things go wrong, *he* alone is responsible. As his sense of responsibility has grown, so has his sense of guilt. Consequently, not only must a parent suffer the burden of a wayward child but he must also live with the feeling that somehow it is his fault, that he could have averted the misfortune.

The truth of the matter is that we still live in a world in which we are at the mercy of many forces. The child has no control over whom it has for parents. Neither do the parents have control over the sex of the child, nor the factors of heredity. It may very well be that as behavioral scientists learn more about humans, they will discover that behavior is controlled more by heredity and body chemistry than we are now aware. (The research of William H. Sheldon on physique and behavior is of particular interest on this subject.[4]) And those of us who have found Christianity to be a meaningful way of viewing life and the world are still convinced that the will of God is working out his purpose through us and in the world.

All of this is to say that parents frequently assume too much responsibility for their children's failures — and successes. Other forces are at work.

Too Much Anxiety?

Some family specialists are beginning to ask whether some types of " help " for parents may in reality do more damage than good. Theories of child rearing have in recent decades moved from the extreme one enunciated by John Watson,[5] who asserted that it is harmful to give a child too much love and attention, to an emphasis on the need for love and physical contact between mother and child. This switching from one emphasis to another can be anxiety-provoking. One student of my acquaintance from the Far East reported that only in recent years had the "modern" practice of bottle-feeding babies filtered into her country. Now, upon visiting this country, she discovered to her dismay that the current trend is back to breast-feeding!

That American parents really want help is attested to by the number of magazines and books offering guidance in child rearing. Parents discussion groups have become common. Family specialists are sought for their "expert" advice. The minister is consulted about the child's religious training, and the pediatrician may dispense more information about the child's emotional state than his physical health.

All these "experts" tend to make parents self-conscious. Possibly they generate more anxiety than they settle. There are times when troubled parents can best be helped by being aided in gaining confidence in themselves, thus allaying their crippling anxiety. Korner feels that professionals have aggravated parental uncertainty by often oversimplifying cause and effect in parent-child relationships, and implying a greater understanding of certain phenomenon than is actually warranted.[6] Such criticism is valid in many instances. It underlines the fact that many factors must be taken into consideration, that a knowledge of the individuals involved is necessary, and that the particular stage of development of the child must all be evaluated. Books and speakers are, of necessity, concerned with generalities. The makeup of a particular child and the temperament of a particular parent are not taken into consideration. For example, the parent may be admonished to speak in a calm voice to the child. This may be effective with a three-year-old child. But with a specific eight-year-old, a calm voice may be interpreted as "Don't take it seriously." Speakers need to encourage parents to read books, listen to lecturers, participate in discussions, and then *use their own best judgment in relating to their children.*

What has been said in this chapter should not be construed

to mean that parents should not seek outside help. There are times when such help is urgently needed. In many cases, a little help at the right time may avert more serious disturbances. Probably the great majority of those who consult specialists about their children really do have a problem that in most instances can be helped with adequate guidance.

Change is always accompanied by self-doubt, anxiety, resentment, and regret, Nelson Foote asserts.[7] A healthy response by modern adults to this problem, he feels, is the growth of study groups, family-living courses, and popularized scientific studies by competent writers. Handled wisely, these are undoubtedly making parents more able to meet the demands of parenthood in a day when their children are living accelerated social lives and when speed is gauged in miles per second, and distance measured in light-years.

8

ACCELERATED LIVING

THE TIME CLOCK might well be a symbol of modern life. We are harassed by schedules. A bus running five minutes late throws many of its passengers into fits of unbearable anxiety. Our forefathers measured time in leisurely terms of seasons or years, months, weeks, and days. Even today the rural church may frustrate its city-bred pastor beyond endurance because the congregation does not mind waiting fifteen or twenty minutes because " the Jones family said they'd be a little late."

But our accelerated living takes other forms. We are used to instant coffee, instant creamed potatoes, and other " instant " items. Many young people, by the time they are thirty, have achieved positions of leadership and financial reward that formerly were won after many years of hard struggle. It is not unusual for a woman to be a grandmother by the age of thirty-five and still have half her life ahead of her.

It is our accelerated living that is the cause of much of the parental anxiety discussed in the previous chapter. Not only are adults living a faster pace of life, but so are their children. Many parents feel that our society is permitting young people to experience at earlier and earlier ages certain freedoms formerly reserved until more maturity was achieved. Numerous family specialists heartily agree. Subteen children, for instance, are increasingly permitted the freedom of privacy in highly

stimulating circumstances. Some authorities say that twelve-
and thirteen-year-old children simply do not have the necessary maturity and self-discipline for coping with their newly
discovered sexual urges. It is not fair, they say, to make the
children solely responsible for curbing their drives. And it is
this fear of sexual involvement which is at the root of most
parental anxiety concerning their subteen and teen-age children. When dating is permitted in grade school, young people,
by the time they are fifteen or sixteen, may feel that everything
has been experienced. In too many instances, it has, and there
is little left to do but get married. American young people
are marrying at increasingly early ages. Since the turn of the
century, men are marrying about three years earlier and
women about two years earlier. At present, the most frequent
age of marriage for men is twenty-one, and eighteen for
women. According to one author, girls who marry in their teen
years, that is, before twenty, are three times as likely to end
up in the divorce court as those who wait until they are
twenty-one or twenty-two.[1] Of course, this does not mean that
a marriage at eighteen is doomed to failure. It simply means
that it is statistically risky. And the risk increases as the age of
marriage decreases.

This chapter will devote itself to exploring some of the factors involved in this speedup of life and the dangers involved
by the tendency of our society to push its young people into
growing up too soon.

There seem to be at least three factors contributing to the
thrusting of young people into premature experiences. Possibly there are others.

The Accelerated Pace of Life

As noted above, the whole of life moves at a dazzling pace
in an atomic era. On a recent from Chicago to New York jet
trip, it took longer to land at the crowded airport than it did
to get there. A trip to the moon covering hundreds of thousands of miles will take a fraction of the time it took Columbus

to cross the few thousand miles of the Atlantic. Perhaps the speedup of life in the physical environment has generalized to other areas. Whether it has or not, it is obvious that there has been an acceleration in the social sphere. Little girls are seen wearing nylon hose although their legs are not yet sufficiently filled out to take the wrinkles out of the hose. Ten-year-old girls complete with lipstick, mascara, and pancake makeup are occasionally seen. "Training bras" are advertised for girls who have no more need for them than their brothers. And their brothers are buying cars, or the parents are giving them the money to buy them, as soon as they are old enough for a license. Some teen-agers drink and smoke. This is nothing new, for teen-agers sneaked out to drink and smoke in previous generations. What is new is that some parents are openly permitting or encouraging this type of "adult" experience. In some circles, both sexes are being encouraged to start dating before they reach the teen years, and dances for subteens encourage the illusion that these children are "little adults."

One parent reported that she did not realize how early her twelve-year-old daughter was starting to date until she dropped the daughter and her thirten-year-old date off at the local movie. As the boy purchased the tickets, she heard him say: "Two. One adult and one child." The parents reconsidered and decided to keep their "child" at home awhile longer.

Of course, any one of the above experiences taken by itself is not of tremendous importance. But collectively they create an illusion in the mind of the child that he is an adult. After all, many children participate in most of the experiences engaged in by adults. Then the parents are horrified to discover that their fifteen-year-old daughter is pregnant or wants to get married. Although there are many factors involved in teen-age premarital pregnancies and/or marriages, one of the causes is the early participation in experiences that make the teen-agers feel older than they are.

One of the tragic aspects of this acceleration is manifested in the stunting of the personality. Dr. Frances Ilg, director of the Gesell Institute of Child Development, has been quoted as saying that each stage of a child's development must be lived through completely in order to prepare adequately for the next.[2] Youngsters who are pushed through one stage too soon, Dr. Ilg continues, are likely to fixate on themselves and their interests. They get confused about sex, love, and life. In short, they may never grow up.

Dr. Margaret Mead expresses her concern in another manner. The trend toward earlier marriages in our accelerated society, she feels, is sheer wastefulness of human personality. It is wasteful not only in terms of the significantly higher divorce rates, but also because of the attendant emotional stunting that may prevent the young people involved from developing into the kinds of persons they would have been otherwise.[3] Perhaps this is another reason why the grandmother in her late thirties is confused and bored. She never had a chance in her teens to discover who she really is. And possibly her husband feels thwarted and cheated in life partly because his premature marriage kept him from achieving his potential or developing his dreams.

SOCIAL PRESSURES

Another source of the forces pushing youngsters into premature experiences is to be found in the social pressures of the society. Here, as in other situations, no one person or group is to blame. The whole society is responsible. The entire culture seems to have conspired together to push the minds of its young people into thoughts of love, sex, and marriage. On every hand and through every media they are bombarded with the philosophy that handsome men and lovely women are irresistibly drawn to each other by sexual appeal, and in the bliss of wedded love and children, all problems are solved. "We have set up marriage and children," says Dr. Judson Landis, "as the panacea guaranteeing happiness and security to every youngster." [4]

In view of the constant selling of sex, romance, and marriage as the cure for all ills, perhaps it is no wonder that many couples are disillusioned by sex and marriage. "Is this all there is to it?" was the shocked reaction of a girl to her first experience with intercourse. It might well be the reaction of many other women. And the evaluation of marriage by a young disillusioned husband could express the feelings of many men. "This marriage bit," he said bitterly, "isn't what it's cracked up to be. They sing about it making you happy," he continued, "but so far as I can see, it is a ring on her finger and a ring in your nose!" Ever since Ernest Burgess wrote his insightful paper on romance in 1926, students of family life have recognized that the romantic buildup of sex, love, and marriage, and the subsequent disillusionment after marriage, are important factors in many marital failures.

Another facet of the social pressures pushing young people into premature experiences is the emphasis on physical appearance. Of course, the youngsters are not the only targets of this propaganda, as a glance at any popular magazine will demonstrate. The feeling is communicated in no uncertain terms that the beautiful girl gets the handsomest boy and vice versa, and the handsomest, best-dressed man gets the quickest advancements in the business world. Face creams, hair sprays, fingernail polish, girdles, bras, perfumes, lipstick, hair tint, eye makeup, deodorants, hair shampoo, cleansing creams, face soaps, and weight-control methods are a few of the beauty devices that take up considerable advertising space in the popular communication media. Boys are little better off, since they are made to feel guilty if their bodies do not ripple with well-developed muscles. Magazines directed at young people offer glowing promises to make musclemen out of scrawny weaklings — the envy of other boys and the object of admiration by every beautiful girl. It is not that some of these are not desirable (I am thoroughly in favor of deodorants!), but rather that an exaggerated emphasis is placed on these relatively superficial aspects of one's life.

This conditioning of the mind to confuse love and sex begins at a rather early age. One of the most common expressions of this is seen every time an adult chucks a five-year-old boy under the chin and says, " Who's your girl friend? " As if a five-year-old boy *ought* to have a girl friend. Certainly this is intended as an innocent remark by the adult, but it does reflect a common attitude on the part of our society.

One of the most insistent pressures confronting young people is that of steady dating. A high school student without a " steady " runs a risk of not going to the next social event at school. But there is also the pressure of being made to feel different, left out, or unpopular, if one is not steady dating. One of the common anxieties that I see in young people with whom I talk arises out of not having a steady. Sixteen-year-old girls without a steady are all too often suffering from fears of being an old maid. " I can't believe anyone will ever really want me," exclaimed one of these fearful girls. A few months later she met her " first love " and four months later they were married, shortly after her seventeenth birthday.

However, the pressures for steady dating do not all come from the peer group. Some of it originates with parents. The tremendous ego involvement of some parents in their children causes the parents to feel unpopular and ostracized if their daughter is not going steady by sixteen. This is particularly true of the socially ambitious middle- and upper-middle-class segments of the community.

Some parents attempt to resist the pressures of the community. This is more easily said than done. One anxious parent, who called her pastor one day, exemplifies this problem. According to her, the school was sponsoring a dance for her daughter's class of twelve-year-olds, and they had all been instructed by the teacher to go home, get on their suits and evening gowns, and return that evening for the dance. This mother and father were of the opinion that twelve is entirely too young to begin ballroom dancing. At the same time the girl, in tears, pleaded: " But, Mother, if I don't go, I will be the only one not there. All the kids, and even the teacher, will be asking me why. How can I tell them the real reason? " The quandary of this parent, and of others in her situation, was: Will it do more damage to press my convictions on her, or let her make her own decision? Each situation has to be weighed individually. However, there are ways in which social pressures can be resisted, and this will be discussed in the concluding section of this chapter.

AMBITIOUS PARENTS

It has already been indicated that the parents themselves are partly responsible for the pressures that their children confront. Someone has observed, with tongue in cheek, that never has a generation of parents given birth to so many gifted, natural-born leaders and child prodigies as the current one. No one has plain kids anymore! This is especially true of the middle class and more particularly of the educated middle class. Even the grandparents are in on the pushing. One grandmother reported that she had a gifted grandson. When an inquiry was made as to what led her to this conclusion she replied, " Well, when the music plays, he sways." Even some parents feel that ordinary toys are not sufficient; it has to be an educational toy! This generation of parents seem overly anxious that their children " have the very best." Perhaps it is partly related to the fact that many of the parents were growing up during the great depression of the 1930's and therefore had so few material advantages and were unable to get the education they desired. Those who have achieved much can never quite forget that they " came up the hard way." This is a point of great pride. Since so few of the current generation are coming up the hard way, one wonders what they will have as their point of pride.

In their desire that the children " have the best," many parents make considerable financial sacrifices in order that their children can attend a prestige private school, take dancing lessons, go to charm classes, and be members of the " right " fraternity or sorority. In fact, one gets the unmistakable impression that the child *has* to succeed. The report card is watched with eagle eye, and grades that do not measure up to parental expectations (usually nothing less than an A or B) bring threats and lectures. One gets the feeling that poor grades can only be a reflection of poor parents.

Some parents, having had a course in psychology, take the positive approach and begin when their child is small, instilling in him the idea that they have confidence in him that he can do anything to which he applies himself. Again and again he is told that he *can* do it. But the truth of the matter is that the child cannot do *everything*. He may not have the intellectual capacity to do superior academic work, regardless of how much the parents encourage him. Those parents who take the positive and those who take the negative approach frequently both fall into a pitfall. The child may eventually reach the point where it seems that, regardless of how hard he tries, he cannot please his parents. If this becomes internalized, the child becomes self-depreciating. In such a case, the parents no longer have to tell him he is failing to measure up to expectations. His own bullying superego does it for them. Even when he does succeed he cannot derive a sense of achievement out of it.

Why do parents so ambitiously push their children? Dr. Judson Landis, along with other students of the family, believes that one of the main reasons is the vicarious satisfaction derived by the parent through their children's achievements.[5] The father who perceives of himself as having been less than the " he-man " type in high school and college is especially likely to be concerned that his son be the hairy-chested football type. Rejection by insecure fathers who perceive feminine qualities in their sons can be thoroughly devastating. The " wallflower " mother may be overly anxious that her daughter be popular. It is not uncommon for a teenage girl to report that her mother with gleeful delight wants to hear all the details of the daughter's date. One of these daughters reported: "I get the third degree when I get in from a date. She wants to know where we went, if he kissed me, where he kissed me, and what he said to me." Why? It could be that this mother is once again reliving her youth, or more likely living it as she wishes it had been.

It is mainly "pushy" parents who promote dances for subteens. "Don't they look cute," remark admiring parents, observing their ten- and twelve-year-olds all dressed up on the dance floor. But a closer look reveals that the parents seem to be enjoying it more than the kids, who feel out of place. "Most boys at that age would rather hug a bottle of castor oil than a girl," quipped one parent. However, it does meet the needs of the parents. There are good reasons why the boys feel this way. One of the reasons is that the girls are at least two years ahead of the boys developmentally. Boys are still at the cowboy-and-Indian stage when girls start thinking of the social graces. Some feel it is painfully unfair to drag these would-be Lone Rangers onto a dance floor.

Can Anything Be Done?

What can be done to combat the forces that are at work pushing children prematurely into adult experiences? It is unfair to expect children to have the necessary ego strength to withstand the pressures brought to bear upon them. Even their parents have a difficult enough time. This problem of what can be done has been one that I have posed to numerous parents' groups with whom I have worked in recent years.

First, parents need to learn to stand together in the face of pressures. When it is asserted that "everybody is doing it," a closer check may reveal that the child is hard put to come up with a specific example. But more than this, parents may need to unite and draw up specific codes of expectations such as was done by the Parents' League of Charlotte, North Carolina.[6] Though controversial, this group has done much to relieve some of the pressures experienced by Charlotte parents. These parents decided to do something when it became apparent that the children, not the parents, were setting the standards of their own social behavior. After considerable study, a series of recommendations for parents, covering various age groups, were suggested. These have been printed in a pamphlet entitled *Let's Agree*. It is circulated and followed by many parents.

David Mace has suggested that parents need to work to change the trend toward earlier and earlier dating. He is of the opinion that fifteen should be the age of beginning to date.[7] If the age is to be pushed back, parents, or at least groups of parents, will probably have to unite to create a uniform code of behavior to minimize youngsters' sense of being different.

Secondly, most parents feel that it is important to gain control of children rather early. Parents who have let their children have a free hand until the teen years, and then try to clamp down when trouble appears on the horizon, are in for a shock. They may be pushing their child into an early marriage or may create a worse problem than the one they are trying to solve. Gaining control is accomplished very early in everyday life experiences. For example, children should have a bedtime schedule rather than be allowed to stay up until *they* decide to go to bed. In regard to food, they should learn to eat what is on the table rather than expect the mother to prepare separate dishes for them. Parents have a right and a responsibility to know where their children are going, as well as to decide whether they may go. Thus, these parents' groups feel that children who learn to follow such reasonable household regulations, and who learn early that parents have a say in their activities outside the home, are children who are going to be more amenable to parental control later on. Children who fail to learn respect for authority in the home usually have trouble relating to authority in the larger world.

Finally, these parents with whom I have worked seem to feel that discussion itself among parents can have a therapeutic effect. Through open discussion, parents can sometimes gain insight into what they are unwittingly doing. Basically, the concern of the modern parent on behalf of his children is healthy. In its exaggerated forms it becomes unhealthy. The concern of a parent for the social development of a child is to be desired. But undue concern that causes parents to push their children into premature experiences can cheat their children out of some of the meaningful experiences of "just being kids."

There are no easy answers to complex social problems. Neither is there an easy answer to this accelerated living of our young people. Many parents, although not promoting such premature experiences, will acquiesce in order to avoid the anger of their children or the scorn of a neighbor. But there is no real way for parents to avoid having their children angry at them at times — if the parents are truly being parents. Parents may not be "liked" at all times by their children, but they should be respected.

9

LONGER YEARS OF RETIREMENT

IF THE ACCELERATED LIFE of young people is one problem of the American family, on the other end of the continuum is another — old age and longer years of retirement. With sixty-five being the compulsory retirement age for a large segment of the population, and the prospects of it being lowered to fifty,[1] our society faces the problem of helping these longer-living adults learn how to make these years meaningful.

Man has long been interested in the process and problems of aging. However, it has not been until recent decades that a more formal, systematic study, called gerontology, has been made of old age. Attention has been forced in this direction because for the first time in human history, older people comprise a significant segment of the population. This, to a large degree, has occurred in our century. The 1961 White House Conference on Aging reported that, in the United States, there are 16,000,000 adults who are sixty-five and over. They comprise approximately 11 percent of the population today, compared to an estimated 4 percent in 1900.[2]

Inasmuch as the pastor appears to spend about one third of his calling time each week with older people,[3] it behooves him to learn as much as possible about old age, its problems and satisfactions, in order for him to enrich his ministry to this group.

THE OLDER PERSON IN A NEW ERA

Many older persons in our industrialized society occupy an awkward position — they are in the way. The men, at least, are arbitrarily retired at sixty-five, their wisdom, experience, skills, and knowledge no longer desired. It appears that the rest of society then becomes primarily concerned with meeting enough of their needs to keep them out of the way so that the wheels of business and industry can grind on — in younger hands. In all societies, people have been forced to withdraw from productive work in the later years, but they withdrew into an honored position with new responsibilities. Their years of experience and wisdom were respected and sought by younger members of the group. The young American tends to look upon older people as " old fogies." Youth, not age, occupies the honored position in our hierarchy of values. It is a time of energy, speed, efficiency, and productivity, all of which are important to an industrialized society. Youth is also a time of beauty and handsomeness. These are also highly valued. " You don't look your age," Max Lerner observes, is one of the most flattering things that can be said to older Americans, " . . . as if it were the most damning thing in the world to look old." [4]

This is not to say that all older people are frustrated and unhappy. In a study of several hundred older adults, it was discovered that most of them found their retirement years to be happy once they moved through a period of readjustment into their new status.[5] In fact, many of these older people found that not having to work so hard, or not having to work at all, was a great relief. However, there are those who find this transition difficult.

The structure of the modern family is not conducive to meeting the needs of older adults. The " ideal " family nowadays includes the husband, wife, and their dependent children. This image of the family leaves no room for the grandfather and/or grandmother. Not only do the children often feel uncomfortable and imposed upon at having to have their parents living with them, but the parents also feel that they should not live with the son or daughter. Even when their presence is desired, and many children enjoy having their parents near, the older person still feels uncomfortable. There was a time when it was an expectation of the society that children care for aging parents in their homes. It was particularly true in patriarchal societies, where this responsibility fell to the eldest son. In Biblical times, this son also received a double portion of the family inheritance.

Another factor that complicates caring for aging parents in one's home is the size of the modern home. Its five or six small rooms are hardly inviting to an older person who would have little room for privacy, and the son or daughter understandably shares this apprehension.

The mobility of the modern family, both geographically and socially, adds to the problems of parents living with the children. For the parent to live with his grown child often means leaving a familiar community and way of life to move to a strange one a thousand miles away. This necessitates not only adjusting to a new locale, but often to social circles entirely foreign, which further isolates and creates discomfort for all concerned. "We could provide Mom a much more comfortable life," said one son, " but she's not used to our way of life, and says she's happier back home with her old cronies." All these factors add to the difficulties in adjusting to the retirement years.

Retirement and the older years do not have the same impact on women as on men. This is true because, for the most part, women continue to have the same responsibilities at home that they always had. Even women who work outside the home and are retired continue to care for the home. Old age is most difficult for men because accompanying it is the cessation, or decline, of several factors from which the man derives his sense of masculinity and meaning. At sixty-five he is forced to retire from his work, his sex drive is declining, his brawny muscles no longer ripple under the skin, he is less active, and he usually spends more and more time ill in bed, with other people waiting on him. These factors attack his security, depending on how much stock he has had invested in each area. Retirement from work is probably the most difficult of these to accept. Retirement for a person who has spent a lifetime deriving much of his sense of significance in productive activity demands a major reorientation of himself. This brings us to three of the most basic problems men confront in retirement.[6] The first is finding something else to do, having given up their job. They usually cannot find the satisfactions that women derive out of sociability for its own sake, and other significant activity is often difficult to find. A second problem has to do with the loss of status identity. Since a family's prestige is closely related to the occupation of the husband, that prestige is weakened if he no longer has an occupation. Of course, this also attacks his own sense of personal prestige. A third problem that retirement poses for men is the loss of a peer group. Few men report maintaining close contact with their former colleagues. Consequently, the retired man is forced to depend on his wife to meet more of his needs for companionship. But the wife is often becoming more and more involved with groups of widows who have lost their husbands and relatives. Furthermore, one of the common complaints by wives about their retired husbands is that they are around the house so much that they " get under foot."

George Lawton notes that among men who seem to make the best adjustments to retirement are two types. One of these is the person who has " always believed that his importance lay in what he is as a person and not in what he owns or whom he can impress." [7] That is, his security has been drawn from a profound self-respect rather than out of the prestige of his occupation. However, this type of maturity is not easily accomplished in a society that communicates the feeling that one is worthwhile only so long as he is useful or productive.

The second type of man is the one who has always liked his house or apartment, who takes an interest in its appearance, who enjoys puttering and making repairs, who can even run the house when his wife is away.[8] Since retirement usually means spending considerable time at home, if he enjoys his home, this can become a source of satisfaction.

MEETING THE NEEDS OF OLDER ADULTS

Ironically, though science has achieved a history-long goal — that of longer life — from a sociological standpoint we are having trouble assimilating these longer-living adults. Herein lies a challenge. Some are saying that since science has added years to our lives, now religion must add life to the years. The aging have at least five basic needs. They need health to enjoy, some place to live, something to do, someone to care, and some philosophy to guide them. It is easier to satisfy the physical requirements than the social and psychological ones. Without necessarily dealing with the five needs, there are three emphases that are basic to a more adequate program of meeting the requirements of adults in the retirement years.

First, more emphasis needs to be given to an educational program of *preparation for old age*. Recent decades have seen hundreds of courses, seminars, and discussions on preparations for family life. Why not have a program of preparation for old age? This should begin early. The best preparation for a satisfying final ten or fifteen years is to live a rich, full life the first sixty-five. After all, people in their older years are simply a continuation of the same persons they have always been physically, mentally, and emotionally. The importance of appreciating each stage of life, including old age, was recognized by Cicero in 44 B.C. In his delightfully current essay on old age, some friends come to Cato, an old man, and remark how well he wears his years. Cato replies:

Men who have no inner resources for a good and happy life find every age burdensome; those who look for all happiness from within can think nothing evil which the laws of nature entail.[9]

Who can foster such a program of preparation for these retirement years? The church occupies a unique position unequaled by any other community organization for ministering to older people. No other agency is so readily accessible or so well known as the church. Furthermore, the retirement years often find older people withdrawing from many community and civic groups, but few drop their relationship with the church, though they may play a less active leadership role. Partly as a result of all this, pastors are increasingly becoming concerned with discovering how to minister more effectively to this significant segment of the population. Accordingly, two excellent volumes on the subject have come from the pens of four authors. The first of these, *Older People and the Church,* by Paul Maves and Lennart Cedarleaf, is the first comprehensive study of its kind. A more recent book, *The Church and the Older Person,* by Robert Gray and David Moberg, includes much original research on religion and the older person, plus numerous practical suggestions. I am indebted to both of these books for part of what is said here.

Old age and death create so much discomfort in the minds of many Americans that we are guilty of dealing with it in the proverbial ostrich head-in-the-sand manner. It is simply easier not to think about it. However, sooner or later a person must face the fact that he is aging. Its awareness may come gradually, or strike like a bolt of lightning: " I am getting old! " A program of preparation for old age should begin by fostering a realistic view of life, one that includes youth and old age, happiness and suffering. Discussion groups might well deal realistically with old age long before a person reaches that vague line dividing middle age from old age.

One of the areas in which our attitudes need educating has to do with the stereotypes about older people. One of these is that *all* older persons are childish. The observation by Maves and Cedarleaf on this point is pertinent:

A childish older person is in reality a person who has never grown up, in the sense that he has never learned how to handle problem situations constructively. Many such persons go through life masking their immaturity under a cloak of conventionality, until they meet a situation which cannot be solved in a conventional way.[10]

Other misconceptions are that older people are all alike: they cannot learn new interests and adapt to new situations; they can no longer be active and contribute to society; they are devoid of sexual interest; it is old age itself which is the problem; and time spent with older people is wasted.[11]

One of the best preparations for the retirement years, so far as the church is concerned, is helping the individual to develop *a deep, meaningful religious faith*. The research of David Moberg indicates that church membership, as such, does not contribute to successful personal adjustment in old age, but religious beliefs and activities do.[12] Again, he found that in comparing two groups of " believer " and " nonbeliever " older people, the personal adjustment of the " believer " group, as measured by a psychological test, was significantly superior.[13]

What has been said here is that adequate preparation for old age is best started in youth or in middle age. He who does not hear the music of life in his younger years is not likely to hear it in his older years.

A second area of need for older persons is *meaningful activity*. This is particularly true of the men who are now retired from their regular occupation. Only a youthful visionary pictures the bliss of old age as being able to sleep until ten A.M. and then arise to enjoy a day of inactivity and absence of responsibility. Good mental health demands that the aging, as well as others, be engaged in purposeful activity. The prospect of the absence of responsibility after a lifetime of productive activity can be a frightening experience. This anxiety is captured in a perceptive passage from the television play *Marty*, by Paddy Chayefsky, which later became an award-winning movie. The author has Aunt Catherine say:

It's gonna happen to you. Mark it well. These terrible years. I'm afraida look inna mirror. I'm afraid I'm gonna see an old lady with white hair, like the old ladies inna park, little bundles inna black shawl, waiting for the coffin. I'm fifty-six years old. What am I to do with myself? I have strength in my hands. I wanna cook. I wanna clean. I wanna make dinner for my children. I wanna be of use to somebody. Am I an old dog to be in fronta the fire till my eyes close? These terrible years, Theresa! [14]

Perhaps the world's largest consumer of volunteer services is the church. No segment of the adult population has more time available for such services than the segment comprising people of retirement age. Therein lies both a challenge and an opportunity, a challenge to the church to make use of these people, and an opportunity for the older persons to engage in meaningful activity. To be sure, what each person can contribute in the way of service depends upon his own abilities, physical health, and the like. Gray and Moberg devote a whole chapter to specific ways in which older people can help their church. These are:

> Participate in worship services
> Engage in personal devotional activities
> Pray
> Teach
> Help in visitation program
> Help maintain the property
> Help with clerical work
> Help conduct church business
> Participate in organized groups [15]

Of course, these activities do not encompass the whole of one's life. Other activity is also needed. But these are certain ways in which older people might find opportunities for meaningful and creative self-expression through the church and thereby render an important service to the Kingdom of God. And as has been observed, any program of aging successfully must include an attempt to be of service to something or someone outside ourselves.[16]

A third area of need in older people is to *belong to some fellowship relevant to the needs of older persons.* One has only to visit a large city to discover many groups whose sole purpose is to bring together older people who are alone and lonely, uprooted, and lost in the morass of modern urban life. Some of these groups appeal to older adults with titles of "The Golden Years Club," "Forty-Plus Club," and the like. Many of the people who join these groups are members of churches. However, they usually have failed to find the church or groups within the church a meaningful facet of their daily existence. The church has not moved beyond being an *organization* to these people to the more profound levels of being an *organism* that cares, feels, undergirds, and heals.

"All alone." These words describe millions who have out-lived friends and relatives and now look around to find themselves alone in the arena of life. Although our industrialized society has not been equipped sociologically and psychologically to deal adequately with older adults, there are many indications that it is maturing in this area. Perhaps the growing concern of the society will help them avoid that feeling of being utterly alone.

10

THE DECLINE OF RELIGIOUS
BASES OF BEHAVIOR

IT REQUIRES no particular sociological acuity to recognize the decline of religious values in the United States. What may not be recognized is that this decline began not recently, but actually several centuries ago in Europe. It even antedates the industrial revolution. A visit to an art gallery will graphically depict the gradual change from the religious subjects that challenged the imaginations of most of the painters of the Middle Ages to the rarity of such subjects in the works of contemporary artists. In fact, if art is an expression of an age, much of the work by present artists leads one to the conclusion that ours is an age of confusion in which people are torn asunder by nebulous but powerful forces!

Although this decline began several centuries ago in Western society, it was relatively gradual until the last century but has accelerated since 1900. The influence of religion once permeated every facet of life, including government, education, philosophy, art, medicine, and family life. The conduct of business, personal, and family life was subject to various strict regulations. The blue laws still on the statute books of most states, though antiquated and largely ignored by law enforcement officials, are a carry-over from the time when religious sanctions controlled what could and could not be sold on Sunday. Many of the customs and regulations that governed family life had religious bases. Religious injunctions covered marriage, roles of family members, use of leisure time, and the conduct of various other activities of family life. Adultery, for instance, was wrong because it was a sin against God, not because one might get pregnant, get caught, or catch a venereal disease, as modern parents might argue. The family has moved so far from a religious basis that a check of three recent volumes on family dynamics, totaling more than a thousand pages, produced a total of approximately one page devoted to the religious aspects of family life.

Although religion continues to be a significant influence in the behavior of many family members, those who work and counsel with people get the distinct impression that other, more secular influences seem to be gaining as determinative factors, even among persons who consider themselves devoutly religious. One of the new gauges for ethical behavior has to do with what might be called a " numerological approach." That is, if it can be demonstrated that most people engage in a particular type of behavior, then it must be right. One of the best examples of this was manifested after the Kinsey reports on sex were published. Some seemed to feel that if most people engaged in, say, premarital intercourse, then this in some way made it right. Another example is that if most men load their expense accounts, then this makes it right. Of course, those adhering to this concept do not need research indicating that the majority of people engage in a practice in order to feel guiltless. If only one third engage in it, then they are " right " with only one third of the populace. Another measure of behavior is expediency. For example, if glossing over a few of the facts will achieve a certain goal, then this too often determines behavior. This person may pat himself on the back for his shrewd business acumen. On the other hand, he may be honest and present all the facts because this is good business practice. In either case, he has operated on a secular value inasmuch as his behavior was not motivated by the fact that such behavior is religiously right or wrong.

To be sure, people have always violated their religious ethics. Wrongdoing is no modern phenomenon. The point here is that behavior of all types, both positively and negatively, is increasingly motivated by nonreligious values. Those who violate their code of ethics, whether religious or secular, will experience guilt, but they are less likely to feel guilty because of a sense of sin than because they have violated a code of society. Few say with the psalmist, " Against thee, thee only, have I sinned, and done that which is evil in thy sight." (Ps. 51:4.) They may feel guilty because they have disappointed their parents, hurt their mate, or violated their own self-concept, but relatively few verbalize feelings of guilt because their behavior violates their religious faith.

The decline of religious codes of ethics has been accompanied by the growth of secular codes. Even the Government now has different groups at work devising various codes of ethics. Chief Justice Earl Warren, of the United States Supreme Court, is quoted as saying in an address at the Jewish Theological Seminary of America that our society now needs a new profession, that of " counselor in ethics." [1]

Reasons underlying the growth of secular influences are somewhat difficult to trace. It seems to be related to at least three movements. The first is the growth of scientific knowledge which in some instances has conflicted with religious ideas held in the prescientific era. Not many would argue now that the world was created in six twenty-four-hour days. The discoveries of astronomy, archaeology, anthropology, psychology, biology, and nuclear physics have all had their impact on religious concepts. All these have tended to undermine the influence of religion. Related to the increase of scientific knowledge, and yet distinct from it, is the development of technology. It has created desires in us for the " things " that technology produces, thereby contributing to a materialistic outlook on life. This has helped to turn more and more attention away from the church which was once the focal point in the community. The automobile, for instance, now makes it possible for young people to meet their needs for social contacts at places other than the church. Television is strong competition for Sunday evening church programs, and the bass in the lake fifty miles away continue to create a challenge to the preacher's sermon on Sunday morning. Beyond the development of science and technology, perhaps there is a third element to be found, which is not directly related to science and technology — a generalized movement toward secularization in the society. In any case, all these have contributed to a decline of the religious orientation of the society.

The growth of secularism has profoundly affected the elements of religion itself. One evidence of this is seen in the increasingly humanistic emphasis in some religious circles. Man, not God, is becoming the measure of all things. This is rightfully disturbing to many theologians. The essence of Christianity is God's redemption of man through Christ. This is the heart of the gospel, they feel, and any attempt to remove it from the central focus will inevitably give rise to a theology in which man rather than God is worshiped.

The growth of secularism has affected religion in another way: by devaluating the role of the pastor. The time was when the pastor was indeed the " parson," for, as many know, the word means " person " and the pastor was *the* person in the community. The physician now occupies the top prestige position of the community and the minister has dropped, depending upon which poll one reads, to one of the lesser-ranking professions. Dr. George Gallup once asked a group of adults: " Suppose a young man came to you and asked your advice about taking up a profession. Which one of the following (assuming he was qualified) would you first recommend to him? " That of clergyman ranked seventh. Only 5 percent of the respondents said that this would be their first choice.[2] As a result of all this, many denominational leaders are distressed by the lack of interest in the ministry on the part of young men, particularly the most promising young men.

Along with the secularization of the pastor's role, functions formerly performed by him are being transferred to other community members. Thus, the funeral director is increasingly offering comfort to the bereaved in *his* chapel, and the guilt-laden are " confessing " to psychiatrists and psychologists who administer their own style of " pastoral care."

As the prestige of the pastor has declined, people have increasingly turned to secular sources for assurance that there is a God. There was a time when, if the " man of God " believed in the Almighty, this was enough to reassure the doubtful. Few people seem to be impressed any longer by the fact that the minister believes in God. He is supposed to. But if an article appears on " Twelve Reasons Why a Scientist Believes in God," this somehow is much more reassuring. Even the minister seems impressed. In some strange way, the scientist's knowledge about science has also bestowed upon him an all-knowing aura of knowledge about the spiritual.

In the Peace Corps, the United States has secularized the foreign missionary. One missionary to Africa reported that their own prestige had noticeably increased with the initiation of the new program. Of course, the interest of the Peace Corps in the health, education, and certain economic aspects of the countries in which it works parallels in many respects the work that missionaries have been doing for a long time. Perhaps it seems a bit more challenging, or " right," if the Federal Government sponsors such endeavors. Also, the image of mission work involving preaching to half-naked natives still persists in the minds of many people.

Paradoxically, while religious values have been declining as an influence in our society, there has been a decided growth of religious interest. This has been particularly true in the years since World War II. If membership in churches, synagogues, and other religious organizations is an accurate index to the depth of religious devotion in our country, then we are a profoundly religious people. The percentage of the

population having church membership in the United States
is as follows:

1920:	43.0%
1930:	47.0%
1940:	49.0%
1950:	57.0%
1954:	60.3%
1955:	60.9%
1956:	62.0%[3]

By 1961, the number of persons belonging to religious bodies
had increased to 63.4 percent, which is quite a contrast to the
16 percent who belonged in 1850.[4]

Although a larger percentage of Americans are church members than ever before in our history, the consensus among the
scholars is that this involves a relatively superficial commit-
ment to religious ideals. It reflects religious interest more than
religious devotion. The religious revival is extensive but not
intensive. It has become both popular and profitable to be
religious. Its popularity is seen in the statistics above. Its
profitability is seen in the rash of religious movies and songs
in recent years. The movies impress many as being more risqué
than religious. And songs that lilt of the "man upstairs" in
jazzy rhythms seem more sacrilegious than sacred.

A striking change is reflected in the character of this new
religion. Generally, it seems to demand and expect little of
its adherents. The best example of this change is seen in the
new terms in which God is conceived. He is no longer a remote,
stern father who punishes evil and rewards good. In fact, this
new God is rather difficult to describe, "not because he is so
remote but because he is so near, cuddled up right next to
us."[5] He has three distinguishable features, according to
Martin Marty.[6] First, he is understandable and manageable.
Heaven has been brought down. There is little in him to
strike the worshiper with wonderment and awe. Secondly, he
is comforting. There is little about this concept of God to
cause discomfort in his presence. He offers a crown but speaks

not of the yoke or the cross. Finally, this new God is " one of us, an American jolly good fellow." He is a buddy, a chum, a good guy who is right next to us. The total effect of all this is the creation of an image of God that some students of religion feel is at best innocuous, and at its worst in danger of lulling its adherents into a fatal spiritual sleep. Proponents of this point of view say they have simply updated the concept of God and interpreted him in terms intelligible to the modern mind. The subtle danger, it seems to me, lies in doing lip service to a concept of God that would lead to a profound religious experience and way of life, while acting on a concept of God that is both an unchristian and an insignificant influence upon one's way of life.

If the society is increasingly being " bleached " of its religious character, and the current revival of religious interest is a superficial excrescence that fails to produce a corresponding moral and ethical behavior, what does this phenomenon mean for the family? Among other things, it means that a greater responsibility is being placed on the family for inculcating in its children those religious values which are important in defining what behavior is legitimate and desirable. The society at large can no longer be depended upon to do this. Of course, many think that this is not desirable, particularly so far as the public-school system is concerned. Although the educational system does embody certain ultimate values of the society,[7] this is not sufficient for those who are interested in more specifically religious values. Generally, Protestantism has supported public education, but, as Wynn and Fairchild observe, " Protestant families have discovered, by and large, that the school cannot be depended upon or expected to foster *their* religious heritage." [8] To be sure, the home is assisted in this task by the church, yet there is evidence that the value system of a child, that which determines behavior, corresponds much more closely to that of the parents than that of the church. Some years ago, Hartshorne and May made a study of the moral attitudes of children compared with various other significant persons in their lives. They found the following correlations:

Parent and Child	.55
Friends and Child	.35
School Teacher and Child	.03
Sunday School Teacher and Child	.002 [9]

This study suggests that parents continue to be the most potent force in molding the attitudes of their children. It also means that the church, to be of much influence on the children, must work through the home.

Although there has been a decline of the religious bases of behavior in our society, and scientific and technological knowledge seems to be outstripping man's social and moral ability to integrate it, there are some who are optimistic about the future. Hector J. Ritey, M.D., consultant to the American Foundation for Religion and Psychiatry, says he believes man's next step in progress may be a breakthrough on the spiritual plane, starting into growth of the now mysterious "silent zone" of the human brain. This could give rise to the next higher stage of ethics and civilization. In his book *The Human Kingdom*,[10] Dr. Ritey asserts that he believes mankind is on the verge of such a development. Time will tell whether or not he is right. Whether such a breakthrough comes or not, the family will continue to be a pivotal agent of religious knowledge and values.

This chapter has observed that with the decline of religious values in the society, behavior has moved from religious to more secular bases. Accompanying this loss of his spiritual center, modern man has increasingly been plagued by a distressing sense of purposelessness or meaninglessness. This has become one of the growing problems confronting those who work with families.

11

INCREASING FAMILY MEANINGLESSNESS

AN INCREASING NUMBER of marriages that end in unhappiness
and divorce are suffering from no particularly definable problem. "Autopsies" of these marriages often reveal no special
pathology such as physical abuse, extramarital involvements,
financial stress, or unusual incompatibility. They simply die.
Such marital "fatalities" often take place among couples who
seem to have the least reason for failure. These couples may
be the very ones who, after several years of hard work, have
at last achieved a modicum of success and are in a position to
relax. Then it strikes, that gnawing sense of dissatisfaction
which eats at the ties binding two people together. It is almost
as if they are unable to tolerate success. For many couples this
is true. A close examination of their distress reveals that the
marriage was killed by that silent killer — boredom. The
struggle to achieve educational, financial, or other goals seems
to have bound the couple together in a common purpose. The
goal being achieved, they have nothing further to bind them
together. It is at this point that what might be called the
"dry rot" sets in. That is, the marriage expires by a slow
withering process rather than over a messy, dramatic situation.
To be sure, this boredom or meaninglessness may lead a mate
into an affair in search of something to give substance to an
empty life.

Upon moving into family counseling a few years ago, I noted this phenomenon and excitedly decided that I had made an original discovery. But as usually happens with my " original discoveries," I found that Aristotle, Freud, and my wife had already thought of the idea. This can become positively discouraging. In this case, it was found that others, Viktor Frankl in particular, had already noted this problem as it relates to people in the throes of personal conflicts. Out of his experiences as a prisoner in a Nazi concentration camp, Dr. Frankl concluded that man is not dominated by the will-to-pleasure as propounded by Freud, nor is he dominated by Adler's will-to-power. Man is motivated, Frankl concluded, by a will-to-meaning. Prisoners, he found, could endure the horrors of the death camp so long as they had some purpose for living. Many of those who lost this sense of purpose committed suicide. A moving account of his experiences in the concentration camp is to be found in his book *From Death-Camp to Existentialism*.[1] The meaning for life could be hate of the enemy, hope of escaping, or, as in Dr. Frankl's case, surreptitiously reconstructing a destroyed manuscript on scraps of paper. Out of his experience he discovered the wisdom in the words of Nietzsche: " He who has a *why* to live for can bear almost any *how*." [2] Dr. Frankl terms his school of psychotherapy " existential analysis," though it is also called " logotherapy." An excellent exposition of logotherapy is to be found in A. J. Ungersma's *The Search for Meaning*.[3]

The problem with many modern marriages is that the couple has lost this *why* to live. Consequently, one or both partners experiences a loss of purpose, of direction, of meaning, to their lives. Many of the people occupying the waiting rooms of psychiatrists' offices are people who are suffering from no definable disease, in the strict meaning of the word. Their basic problem is what Frankl calls an " existential vacuum." Their problem has become one of the major challenges to psychiatry, he asserts.[4]

This problem has been the object of growing concern to

Christian scholars. A central focus of the Christian message is that life has a purpose, that history is moving toward a goal, and that God is in charge of history. Countless previous generations have found, in the Christian world view, a sense of ultimate purpose and meaning that many of the present generation, including Christians, have lost. It is to the task of rediscovering this Christian sense of meaning that Émile Cailliet addresses his book, *The Recovery of Purpose*.[5] Having lost its sense of ultimate purpose, our age has reverted to a pessimism and fatalism that prevailed in ancient cultures and continues to pervade contemporary primitive societies.[6] Life to many is "a tale told by an idiot" and man is a helpless pawn in the hands of fate. This fatalism is reflected in much of the contemporary arts. "What used to be a 'Pilgrim's Progress' has become in our time a 'Long Day's Journey into Night,'" to quote Cailliet again.[7] Dr. Cailliet goes on to note that Eugene O'Neill's drama practically tells itself, once certain antecedents of the play are known, for it seems as if there could be no other way it might have happened. Fate has assumed control. He observes: "There is no room for Providence in this pattern of fate and doom. And this is fatalism in a new key — a fatalism all the more tragic because it reasserts itself in a Christian climate."[8] The success of the play lies mainly in the fact that its message speaks to our age.

EXPRESSIONS OF FAMILY MEANINGLESSNESS

If our age has lost its sense of ultimate meaning, how does this loss manifest itself in everyday life? If someone asked the average man on the street whether he suffers from meaninglessness, he would probably think his questioner was an escaped psychiatric patient. Yet the fact that he does suffer from meaninglessness manifests itself in realistic, but subtle, ways.

First, it expresses itself in much of the marital unhappiness and divorce mentioned at the beginning of this chapter. Charles and Alice Kelly, as we will call them, are representative of this group. Alice worked to help put Charles through college and when he later set up his business, she worked alongside him doing all the office work. Their children were born, which made her work more difficult, but she continued. These were years of struggle, but they were happy as they dreamed of "getting on top" and being able to buy a home, nice furniture, and other things young couples desire. The business flourished, and the house and furniture were bought. A cabin on the lake, two cars, a boat (sitting in one side of the two-car garage), fine clothes, and membership in the country club were also acquired. At this point Charles began to drink more heavily and began to criticize his wife about things that had never seemed to bother him before. There was talk of divorce. Even he was puzzled by his behavior, since there was no real reason for their unhappiness. Once he remarked that they seemed to do better when they had less. The truth of the matter is that by the age of thirty-two he had achieved every goal he dreamed of — wife, children, education, successful business, home, and the admiration of friends. He had climbed the highest mountain and there seemed to be no higher one in sight. Now he was bored. Since, in the American mind, marriage is the panacea that cures all ills, he concluded that the problem lay in his marriage. Some men at this stage decide they are in love with someone else. Fortunately for Charles and his wife, they were able to work out their difficulties as he developed insight into himself, and together they discovered new purpose in life.

There is reason to believe that many unhappily married individuals who become emotionally involved with someone else, and who become irritable, critical, or otherwise discontented, may, in reality, be suffering from a lack of purpose that gives direction and meaning to their lives. This leads them into troublesome behavior, perhaps in an attempt to give substance to their empty lives.

Secondly, family meaninglessness expresses itself in much of the mad, frantic "busyness" of American family members. Clubs, fund drives, committees, parties, and religious, educational, and cultural groups all demand, and get, the energies of old and young alike. A sizable percentage of these activities could be abandoned and their services not be missed. Behind much of the mania for organizations and the seeking of pleasure lies a search for a sense of meaning and purpose in life.

Thirdly, meaninglessness expresses itself in the pessimism that pervades some families. This may be manifested in a general sense of frustration over life as verbalized in the words of one wife: " To blazes with civilization! Who ever saw a Hottentot going to a psychiatrist? " It may express itself in the dismal comfort one father found over having all daughters and no sons. " At least I'll not have one worry," he remarked. " I left a part of me in Korea, [a leg] and I'll never have to lie awake at night worrying about them going to war." Other parents express concern about bringing children into a world that they feel sure will ultimately be consumed in a fiery atomic conflagration.

Fourthly, meaninglessness is expressed in much of the behavior discussed in the chapter on unfulfilled women. These are women who fail to find in their everyday work within the home a sense of purpose, meaning, and significance that good mental health demands. One of these wives verbalized her feelings by saying, " I feel like an unfinished symphony." Another said: " I feel like a column of figures that needs totaling. There should be something that will sum things up, bring the various strands of life together. I don't have that."

Finally, family meaninglessness is expressed in the listless, wandering, and often destructive behavior of teen-agers. Of course, a certain amount of this seeking is a normal developmental aspect of adolescence. At the same time, some of their behavior seems to be attributable to a lack of any real sense of purpose in which to channel their energies. They report moving from one drive-in to the next, seeking some type of excitement. A tour around a large city will find numerous teen-agers listlessly " tooling around " at two and three o'clock in the morning. Those in large cities, such as New York, may collect on the streets or doorways with nothing to do. A group of these youngsters once broke into my car in New York and later wrecked it in a wild chase across town. They later reported that they did not know why they did it except that they didn't have anything else to do.

If the American family has lost its sense of meaning and purpose, what has contributed to its decline?

What Happened to Meaning?

In attempting to account for responses in a society, one must constantly bear in mind that there are seldom any single-cause phenomena. Several influences usually converge to produce an effect. Furthermore, cause and effect are interrelated. This is certainly true of the problem of meaninglessness. Nonetheless, certain elements in the society are distinguishable as contributing to the problem.

Scientific and technological advances have been foremost in contributing to the growth of meaninglessness. As Cailliet asserts, science has largely restricted itself to the outlook of the natural man which has thrown an "iron curtain" around him and especially within him.[9] In the minds of many people, science has eradicated the spiritual facet of man. The determinism of science leaves little room for a sense of cosmic purpose. The universe, "Scientism" asserts, is operated by systematic but blindly purposeless forces.

The rapid development of technology has given man control over many of the forces that once terrified him. For instance, few would now see in illness an attempt by God to punish some wrongdoing. Modern man sees sickness as the result of specific causes, many of which science has helped him to control. He has confidence that an almost omnipotent science will conquer other forces that still plague him. This has created a tacit feeling in the minds of many that man has outgrown his need for God. Man, through science, is now in control of his environment, not God.

Another aspect of the growth of technology is that the kinds of activities that formerly contributed to a man's sense of significance and purpose have been changed, and nothing of equal significance has replaced them. The automated assembly line has shrunk the significance of man to where he has difficulty having a sense of achievement at the end of the day. Furthermore, automation has given him more off-work time, and he is having difficulty filling it with significant activity. Technology also has removed production from the home, and this has diminished the home's importance.

The net effects of science and technology have been to help push off the scene a sense of ultimate purpose in the workings of history and the activities of man.

A second factor in the loss of meaning is the decline of religious values in our society. Science may tell us *how* the world operates but not *why*. It is only religion that provides an answer to the meaning that lies behind all of this. When men lose their spiritual values, they are likely to get lost in the midst of life. Even Freud recognized the significance of religion as a force that gives direction and purpose to life. In his *Civilization and Its Discontents* he says: " Only religion is able to answer the question of the purpose of life. One can hardly go wrong in concluding that the idea of a purpose in life stands and falls with the religious system." [10] In fact, the matter of a sense of purpose is so central to religion that W. T. Stace has emphasized that religion can withstand the discovery that the earth is not the center of the universe, that the earth is hundreds of millions of years old, and a host of other discoveries. However, religion " cannot survive destruction of belief in a plan and purpose of the world, for that is the very heart of it." [11] The horizons of modern man have been continually broadened, but his inner horizons, the spiritual, have been shrinking. As a result, he has become lost.

While religious values have been declining in the society, religion also seems to have suffered in another way: through doubt. Doubt here refers not to the doubt that opponents of religion have, but to the doubt that its very adherents have.

Many people seem to have lost faith in the efficacy of their own religion. The question mark is, in too many instances, replacing the cross as the symbol of American religion. One gets the distinct impression that many religious Americans know more about what they do *not* believe than what they *do* believe. Religious values often appear to be held rather tenuously and religious convictions are easily compromised. Concepts of right and wrong are hazy and consciences are easily appeased.

Young people in many churches fail to find in their religion the challenge of a cause worthy of their best efforts. Perhaps they would agree with the hero of *Look Back in Anger* when he says that there are no longer any big, brave causes to champion. At least there are none with which their religion confronts them. Of course, this does not mean there are no longer any big, brave causes; it may simply mean there are no longer any big, brave people to challenge wrongs that need righting, ignorance that needs dispelling, and suffering that needs alleviating. And in doing this, such men see it as a part of the fulfillment of their responsibilities to the Kingdom of God.

If secular values that have little or no concern with ultimate meaning have replaced religious values in the lives of people, and if the religion many do espouse is of an anemic quality, it is no wonder that meaninglessness has overtaken family members.

A third contributing factor to the growth of meaninglessness is that many Americans have lost touch with their roots. That is, urbanization, mobility, and the change in values have uprooted people from the firm, secure soil of those who grow up and live in the same or similar communities with similar values, mores, and folkways. We are potted plants, not those planted in "mother earth." In large cities, people become isolated. Contact with relatives often is rare. There is little sense of being related to the past. Few sons follow in their fathers' footsteps vocationally. All this is involved in having lost touch with our roots. Lacking this rootage, a person is likely to drift.

Howard Halpern is of the opinion that American parents are alienating themselves from one of the most significant sources of meaning — parenthood.[12] Parenthood is also a part of our rootage. He sees a certain danger in parents' relinquishing too many of their responsibilities to various institutions, youth groups, summer camps, and the like. This has left parents remarkably free, but free for what? Lacking the growth-producing effects of parenthood, adults, he feels, may simply fixate at the level of a narcissistic self-concern and frantically join various groups in an effort to be deeply related to something. That is, the vacuum of meaninglessness moves in upon them.

A final source of meaninglessness seems to be related to easily achieved materialistic goals. The young couple mentioned earlier, Charles and Alice, is illustrative of this group. By the time Charles was thirty-two, he had achieved almost every goal of which he had dreamed: wife, children, home, education, luxuries, position, security. What more that was important could he want? To be sure, this is why many couples are happy so long as they are having to struggle. Although they may lack deeper ties, they at least have their struggling to give them a sense of purpose. Somehow in a day when materialistic goals seem to be paramount, there needs to be a rediscovery of the spiritual that lies beyond and beneath such goals. Otherwise, we will continue to experience this type of meaninglessness.

These, then, are some of the factors at work in producing family and personal meaninglessness — growth of science and technology, decline of spiritual values, loss of touch with our roots, and easily achieved materialistic goals. Can modern families recapture their sense of purpose?

THE RECOVERY OF PURPOSE

An increasing number of scholars are concerned in one way or another with the problem of meaninglessness. Some are concerned only to the extent to which they have concluded that life has no purpose. Others, such as Émile Cailliet and A. J. Ungersma, who were mentioned earlier in this chapter, are convinced that the way to meaning lies in rediscovering certain Biblical truths and of reestablishing divine purpose at the center of life. The recovery of purpose is basically a religious one. Freud's statement about this has already been quoted. Other men of stature also assert the same thing. As long ago as 1933, Carl Jung perceived the importance of the spiritual in a sense of purpose.[13] Viktor Frankl emphasizes the same point.[14] Perhaps a theologian should be quoted on this point lest this writer appear to be overly impressed by secular scholars speaking on spiritual topics, a practice somewhat deplored in the chapter on the decline of religious values. In addressing himself to the subject of meaninglessness and the spiritual, Paul Tillich uses these words:

The anxiety of meaninglessness is anxiety about the loss of ultimate concern, of a meaning which gives meaning to all meanings. This anxiety is aroused by the loss of a spiritual center, of an answer, however symbolic and indirect, to the question of the meaning of existence.[15]

The matter of inculcating values and altering attitudes is too complex, and too little is known about the processes whereby this is accomplished to attempt to outline a program for recovering our sense of purpose. The need for it can be underlined, and an idea or two suggested that might offer some direction as to the way we should go.

Those who say that the recovery of purpose is a religious matter do not necessarily mean the Christian religion. However, for those who have found the way of Christ meaningful, the way to meaning lies in the direction of developing deeper dedication to Christ and his cause, in trying to extricate themselves from the materialistic emphasis that obscures the spiritual, in giving more than lip service to their faith, in translating into everyday life those principles and ideas which he taught.

In *The Waste Makers,* Vance Packard indicates the spreading materialism of our day. He opens his book with a dedication: " To my mother and father, who have never confused the possession of goods with the good life." After holding the mirror up to our society for a depressing reflection, he concludes the book with a list of higher priorities, " that most of us might feel better about our lives." This list, it seems, involves certain concepts and ideals in harmony with the Christian spirit. They are:

Greater humility and idealism.

At least occasional dedication to the problems of people beyond the walls of our home.

Deeply cherished personal goals.

A judicious attitude toward the values receivable from personal possessions.

Strongly held personal standards on what is good and evil.

Strongly held personal standards on what constitutes success and failure for ourselves.[16]

As is recognized, these are basically values that are best developed at home. Yet it is difficult to inculcate these concepts in the lives of children when the society as a whole operates on other values. Parents can at least be aware of their own behavior. Inconsistency is so subtle. As one father reported: " I decided we were really going to ' put Christ in Christmas.' But before I knew it, I found myself rushing around buying as feverishly as anyone."

A person needs some type of faith to tie him down. " People are like balloons," said one wife. " If you don't tie them to something, they drift away into the vast sky of nothingness." This person shortly decided that, lacking something to anchor her, she had manufactured such ties out of her worries. That is, she organized her life around her worries. She *needed* to worry. Perhaps this accounts for much of the neurotic worrying among husbands and wives. Given a sense of purpose, even the illness of one of the children, the parents often will abandon their worries and organize themselves around the child. On other occasions, ministers see the lives of those who rediscover their faith, or perhaps discover for the first time the sense of meaning and purpose that Christianity provides, take on a whole new quality. Meaning has been recovered.

12

FAMILY ISOLATION

THE GROWING FAMILY meaninglessness discussed in the previous chapter is, to a large extent, rooted in the isolation of the contemporary American family. To be sure, our families are not isolated physically, for urban areas find house jammed up against house, and millions of people live stacked on top of one another in apartments. Paradoxically though, the closer families are to one another physically, the more detached and isolated they are insofar as an underlying sense of relatedness is concerned. A large city is the loneliest place in the world. As one lonely old lady who used to sit each afternoon on the steps of Union Theological Seminary in New York City said: "Strange, isn't it? Thousands of people all around, and yet I'm all alone." Isolation, then, as used in this chapter, refers to the absence of deep and enduring relationships. One can stand in the crowd at Grand Central Station and be alone in this sense. A discussion of isolation is most relevant to urban life because persons living in smaller villages and rural areas are more likely to have the kinds of ties that make this problem less urgent.

Many modern families are detached from deep, meaningful relationships to other families. Within the breasts of multitudes of these people lies a vast, empty chasm of loneliness. Family members may become "joiners" and feverishly dash about town to this and that meeting as they try to feel a part of something significant. The inner sense of isolation leads others to constantly chatter like monkeys in a cage in an attempt to create an illusion of relating. Others cannot stand the solitude of walking along the street alone, but must have the company of a pocket transistor radio blaring away, which helps them to escape their sense of being alone.

What lies behind the isolation of our families?

SOME ROOTS OF ISOLATION

The roots of isolation, like the roots of a tree, are manifold. Paul Tournier traces the loneliness of modern man (loneliness and isolation are so closely related as to be almost synonymous) to our spirit of competition, independence, possessiveness, and a distorted sense of justice.[1] The sources of isolation to be dealt with here appear to be related to the industrialization of a society.

The *mobility of the family* is a prime contributing factor to the psychological isolation experienced by family members. It is difficult to develop a profound sense of belongingness and relatedness to people whom one has known only a short time in a community to which one has only recently moved. A kind of relatedness grows out of living in a community all of one's life which cannot be developed when families move as often as a large percentage of Americans do. The friends these families have are often merely acquaintances, though they call them friends. It takes years to grow a friend in the deepest meaning of the word.

Not only does the American family move about geographically but it is socially mobile. The upwardly mobile middle class often find themselves thrust into communities and associations whose way of life is quite foreign to the one in which they grew up. It is understandable that they often have a vague sense of strangeness in these situations. This can become an isolating factor, for it impairs opening up to relate to another human being. Instead of relating, one may develop defensive patterns of withdrawing, criticalness, bragging, name dropping, and other mechanisms that isolate one human from another.

One of the most graphic illustrations of family isolation is to be seen in the funeral processions that pass through a city. Even the death of an important person may involve only a few cars in the procession. Sometimes there are no more than two or three. On the other hand, the death of a four-month-old baby in a small rural area can call forth such a large number of people that it would appear to an outsider that the community's leading citizen had died. Not only does one live in isolation in large cities, but one dies in isolation, and is buried in a cemetery tended by strange hands.

This is not to long for the "fleshpots" of an age that cannot be recalled, but, rather, to say that a sense of belonging is difficult to achieve in cities. However, there are those urban families who do have these roots of belonging. One couple recently moved back into an older, and somewhat declining, neighborhood, saying that they both had grown up there and enjoyed the sense of security derived from living there. Others are discovering new ways for meeting their needs for belonging and these will be discussed at greater length in Part III.

The *success philosophy* of many Americans contributes to their isolation. From the time a child is small, the parents begin to inculcate the idea that they have high expectations of him. If Junior is not successful in walking at the prescribed time, the parents become anxious. Their anxiety over future failures in grades, making the team, losing fights, and making friends is apparent. In fact, the whole society demands that Junior succeed and this success is rewarded with grades, medals, scholarships, and other tangible evidences of approval. Upon reaching adulthood, he learns that success brings further approval in the form of promotions and pay increases.

There is nothing particularly wrong with success as such. Were it not for certain successes, humanity would still be living in caves. The danger lies in success being elevated to

something akin to a god at whose shrine one worships. Under
these circumstances, one *has* to succeed. One's worthwhileness
as a person becomes related to whether or not he is successful.
This is another way of saying that a person is worth loving
only so long as he is achieving. A failure becomes a blow to
the very foundations of life itself.

The end result of all this is that barriers are constructed
that increasingly isolate a person. The barrier of fear of failure may prevent him from opening up and relating to another, lest his supposed weakness be discovered. If he fails, the
ensuing sense of personal unworthiness can short-circuit his
relationships. The competitiveness that comes out of a need
to achieve may lead him into a critical attitude, a need to be
always right, or achieving at the expense of others. All these
isolate a person.

A *fear of relating* to another is a third isolating factor. Marriage is the most intimate of all human relationships. It can
provide some of the most deeply meaningful experiences
known to mankind. But its very closeness also means it is
potentially one of the most dangerous relationships. To open
up in love and trust demands more courage than some have.
It is at this point that isolating barriers come into play — the
fear of being hurt, fear that one's weaknesses will be discovered, fear of the disclosure of one's inadequacies, or fear of
revealing one's secrets. In short, this person seems to be afraid
to relate to another. This very fear isolates these persons from
deeper involvements with fellow humans, though they may
inwardly long for them.

In all walks of life, one finds persons who have fears of relating. However, it seems to me that they show up in dispro-
portionate numbers among traveling salesmen and men with
similar occupations. These are men who appear warm and
friendly. They like to be with people, and their outgoing personalities lead a person rather quickly to feel as if he had
known them a long time. However, a closer look at these men
reveals that a large percentage of them are unable to sustain

or tolerate long-term, close relationships. But their work does
not demand close relationships, and one reason they enjoy
it is that they can " pop in, pop off, and pop out," to quote
one of them. A closer evaluation also reveals that even when
the opportunities for close personal relationships arise, they
never really let others into the inner sanctuaries of their being. In brief, their apparent ability to carry on meaningful
relationships can be done only on more superficial levels. The
barriers they construct between themselves and their wives are
often rather transparent attempts to keep the wives from
getting really close to them. A close relationship is threatening. Perhaps it is this type of person to which Guntrip refers
when he says that some people are too afraid to love.[2] But
the person who is too afraid to love is isolated.

ISOLATION AND OUR FAMILIES

The various isolating factors at work on the American family have been instrumental in bringing about certain changes.
One of these is that the family has been thrown more and
more back upon itself to meet its needs for intimacy. This is
a central theme in Gibson Winter's book *Love and Conflict*.[3]
The contemporary family usually consists of the husband,
wife, and their dependent children. After the children are
gone, usually scattered over the country as if they had been
shaken from a saltshaker, only the husband and wife remain.
The mobility of families means that they often live long dis-
tances from relatives. It also means that one may not have had
time to develop the kind of friends who are able to share
deeply in each other's lives. Were the " friends " to whom we
say " drop in some time " to accept the invitation, the startled
look on our faces would graphically depict how much of
strangers we really are. The relatively few friends in the
neighborhood and at work more and more cause the family's
need for intimacy and affection to be channeled through
fewer and fewer people. This ingrownness of the contemporary family means that when something in the relationship

goes awry, the impact is rather urgent, since one has few other sources for emotional sustenance.

Since our isolation has thrown us back upon one another for the satisfaction of our need for intimacy, new burdens have been added to marriage and family life. Marriage is now expected to meet nearly all the needs for companionship, affection, relatedness, and meaning. To be sure, friends and relatives still meet some of these needs, but the marriage relationship is increasingly being expected to bear the load of these needs. Some rather sterile marriages are maintained simply because one or both mates have been able to find other meaningful relationships outside the family. But this is difficult to do in the strangeness of large cities. " Incompatibility " divorces are often another way of saying that the mate has been unable to meet these needs for intimacy. In view of the new burdens of marriage, it is understandable that there is a higher incidence of divorce today than formerly. Marriage is expected to accomplish more.

The hungering for intimacy propels some persons into marriage, as they seek to escape their isolation. An unfortunate aspect of these marriages is that the intensity of their need leads to unwise, premature choices. Those who marry earliest are often those young people who do not have the emotional maturity to sustain the type of intense relationship that marriage entails. When conflict arises — and intimacy inevitably involves conflict — the same hungering that led to the marriage may now propel the couple into divorce as they hastily seek to meet their needs in new loves.

The isolation of the family gives rise to other problems. Out of a sense of loneliness and isolation, a parent may cling to a child with a possessive spirit. In fact, there have been some instances in which it seemed to me that a mother initiated divorce action in order to clutch the children even more closely to her breast, without competition from the father. In other cases, the parents may curry the favor of the children with gifts and indulgent discipline. In either situation, the parents seek that intimacy in relationships with their children which they have failed to find in the marriage.

Some of the sexual problems experienced by modern couples are expressions of their isolation and distance from each other. Intercourse, apart from whatever biological drive is present, represents concern, warmth, a giving of one's self to the other, mutuality. A sense of aloneness, of isolation from the mate, robs the sexual act of its underlying meaning. It therefore becomes an empty experience.

There are two " fatal diseases " that are associated with excessive isolation or loneliness, according to Winter.[4] Perhaps these should be mentioned here. The first is that the isolated person develops deep fears. A person becomes anxious and fearful when isolated. Fears have a way of turning into hates. These may become projected onto others. " They " then become the reason for my problems. Although this alienation contributes to much of our racial and religious tensions it seems to me that it may also account for some family unhappiness. In this case, the mate, in-laws, or another relative becomes the object of contempt.

A second problem arising out of excessive isolation is that a person may be driven to join any group that will accept him. Consequently, a teen-ager may join a gang of juvenile delinquents simply because it accepts him. It may lead others into the " safe " haven of totalitarian movements that offer acceptance. So far as families are concerned, perhaps this accounts for the husband who hangs out at the corner bar, much against his wife's desires. He may admit that his friends are not the most savory characters, but at least he feels accepted there. This need for acceptance may lead wives into joining groups that the family might dislike, as did the woman who joined a radical religious sect and maintained her membership in it even though she and her husband became strangers in the same house. Also, the failure to experience a sense of acceptance from the mate is at the root of many extramarital affairs. These often begin innocently enough: " We have to eat lunch; why don't we eat together? " This proves to be a pleasant experience. Before long the two are looking forward to lunch, and then they plan ways to be together, such as a cup of coffee after work. By then the involvement is well rooted.

If the modern family is isolated, is there hope for escape from this isolation?

ESCAPING FAMILY ISOLATION

If isolation is an expression of the lack of meaningful relationships, then escape from this lonely existence would seem to lie in the direction of relatedness. Only as a person is able to take courage in hand and dares to relate to another person in an I-Thou relationship can the two span the dividing barriers between them. In such an encounter of concern and trust is the Biblical koinonia established.

Translating this into everyday experiences of the family, Tournier notes that every grievance between two people sets up barriers that can be dissolved only by fellowship.[5] Thus, if a husband is hurt because he felt rejected by his wife the previous evening, a barrier has been constructed. To attack his wife only succeeds in forcing her to defend herself by withdrawing or attacking. Even if rejection had not been originally intended by the wife, his attack may put her in a position of rejecting him now. He could say nothing, but this fails to quench the flames of rejection burning within him. He feels cut off, angry. What is he to do? The way out of this isolating experience lies in the ability of these two people to relate to each other in love and concern. Out of such experiences people may learn that the opposite of love is not hate but isolation.

A significant aspect of this healing fellowship between husband and wife, or parent and child, is a willingness to listen. Feeling misunderstood isolates us. This means that overcoming isolation and loneliness involves the ability to communicate, to commune, with another. This type of listening listens for the meanings and feelings that lie behind words. It involves an ability to hear with what Theodor Reik calls the "third ear." [6] The paramount importance of this type of listening is caught in a perceptive passage by Taylor Caldwell in *The Listener:*

The most desperate need of men today is not a new vaccine for any disease, or a new religion, or a new "way of life." Man does not need to go to the moon or other solar systems. He does not require bigger and better bombs and missiles. He will not die if he does not get "better housing" or more vitamins. He will not expire of frustration if he is unable to buy the brightest and newest gadgets, or if all his children cannot go to college. His basic needs are few, and it takes little to acquire them, in spite of the advertisers. He can survive on a small amount of bread and the meanest shelter. He always did.

His real need, his most terrible need, is for someone to listen to him, not as a "patient," but as a human soul. [7]

Although this type of listening establishes a relationship from which strength can be derived and in which healing can take place, there is a profound sense in which one can never entirely escape his isolation. To be human is to be lonely. Ultimately, each person has to live his own life in the solitude of his inner world. There is also a type of aloneness that is creative. In a world filled with people madly rushing about, noise, and dog-eat-dog competition, we need more of the creative aloneness referred to in the Biblical admonition, "Be still, and know that I am God" (Ps. 46:10).

PART III

———

SOME AREAS OF STRENGTH IN THE
MODERN FAMILY

———

13

THE STRENGTHENED ROLES
OF FAMILY MEMBERS

THUS FAR THIS BOOK has basically concerned itself with some of the emerging problems of the modern family. But is the modern family confronted with nothing but problems? Is there nothing to be encouraged about? Are there not some strengths emerging out of the decay of old traditions and the birth of new ones? We believe the answer is an emphatic " Yes! " This section of the book proposes to address itself to certain strengths of the contemporary family.

One of the legitimate complaints leveled on occasion at behavioral scientists is that they seem to be preoccupied with abnormal behavior and with the problems of society. Most people, fortunately, are quite " normal." Some scholars, such as A. H. Maslow, have challenged the use of what he calls " cripple-psychology " to understand healthy people.[1] One can best understand healthy persons by studying healthy, or what he calls " self-actualized," persons. This point of view provides a corrective influence to an overinvolvement in the problems of mankind. This chapter is concerned with the healthier expressions of the modern family.

Perhaps students of the family have tended to concern themselves too exclusively with limitations of the modern family. This book does not want to make the same mistake. It is true, however, that a clear understanding of the problems one confronts must precede any intelligent, constructive effort at bringing order out of chaos. One of the recent challenging studies of healthy families is reported in the book *Successful American Families* by Zimmerman and Cervantes. They express the need for a positive approach to the difficulties of the family by asserting: " We are not going to find the solution to the problems of the new and coming era by increasingly wallowing in the mire created by the outdated one." [2]

Someone has observed that most things are as potentially helpful as they are dangerous, and conversely. This is true of the family. Like the mythical phoenix of old that was resurrected out of the ashes of its fiery destruction, this is happening to the family. This is to say that the strengths of the modern family are also a part of its problems. Florence Kluckhohn says that three major problems of our society are: a confused definition of the feminine role, faulty husband-wife relations, and questionable parent-child relations.[3] But at the same time that she underlines these problems, she is also putting her finger on emerging new strengths of the family: the new role of women, new husband-wife relations, and new parent-child relations. To be sure, there are times when it is difficult to distinguish between the problem and the strength. Perhaps it is analogous to walking a tightrope. But it is a tightrope which Part III will attempt to walk.

THE NEW ROLE OF MEN

The new roles of both men and women in modern society call for a broader participation and experience in the affairs of the family. This is a strength. The role of the man in a patriarchal society was defined as being pretty much outside the home. The King James Version of the Bible aptly describes the role of the wife when it says that women are to be " keepers at home " (Titus 2:5). The literature frequently depicts the patriarchal father as being reserved and rather aloof from his family, much as an army officer is in regard to the men in his charge. If this is an accurate representation, the modern father is quite a different breed of man.

The emerging new man is vitally interested and he actively participates in the home. It is a compliment to a man nowadays to call him a "family man." This signifies stability, among other things. This man feels it is no threat to his masculinity to help with rearing the children, whether this means changing the diapers or getting the children ready for bed. "I would feel cheated," said one of these fathers, "if I could not participate in this way in their growing up." Clinical observation seems to indicate that modern husbands who feel strongest against helping their wives with the children are also likely to express in other ways their masculine uncertainty.

On weekends, especially, the modern husband may do some of the cooking. In fact, cooking outside on the grill seems to be becoming defined as part of the masculine role. He also enjoys "puttering" around the house. This husband derives real satisfaction from being with, and doing things with, his family. Nelson Foote notes that probably the current urban husband spends more time with his wife than husbands did in any decade since production was moved out of the home. Furthermore, it is becoming improper to invite only the husband or wife to events.[4] This trend is alarming to some observers and the term "househusband" is being used to describe the new man's strong home orientation. Margaret Mead has repeatedly expressed the opinion that the modern husband is too domesticated. He invests so much of his emotional energies in the home, she feels, that he does not have enough left to tackle the problems confronted in his work. His domestication has robbed him of his love for the daring and adventuresome, the kind of thing that made explorers out of men from past generations. Dr. Mead notwithstanding, it appears to me that more problems are created in our society by men who care too little for their families than too much. But perhaps she is talking of extreme cases. In fact some authorities are of the opinion that in this "domestication" of the modern husband and father lies the strength of his new role. J. M. Mogey is of the opinion that in recent years there has been a reversal, in some circles at least, of the remoteness of the father from affairs of the family.[5] There is evidence that many fathers are increasingly becoming involved in the intimate daily life of the family, giving it new stability. He notes the steady decline of the divorce rate since 1946 and believes one of the main factors in the decline is the emergence of a significant core of stable families in the society. This stability is based on the redefinition of the father role. As the pattern of father-involvement spreads to the society as a whole, there should be a growing family stability and decline of the divorce rate.

The new role of modern men permits them to express emotions hitherto considered unacceptable in a man. Warmth, gentleness, and tenderness have been added to his repertory of acceptable emotions. These had been considered feminine until now. Some persons still consider them so. The classification of such gentle emotions as also being masculine probably began in the educated middle class. But popular media are beginning to transmit such ideas to the public at large. Thus *Coronet* a few years ago carried an article entitled "Tenderness: A New Style in Masculinity."[6]

Another positive element is the reevaluation that is taking place as to what emotional responses comprise masculinity and femininity. Irene Josselyn, in a provocative article on the psychology of fatherliness, challenges the idea that there are emotions experienced by women that are distinctively feminine, and that any man experiencing the same ones is *ipso facto* feminine. She feels it would be more accurate to assume that an emotion like tenderness is a healthy maturation of certain emotional patterns of all adults. This is expressed in women as motherliness and in men as fatherliness.[7] In short, the same emotional responses are common to both men and women. The culture determines how these shall be expressed.

Our culture seems to be making it possible for men to express more forthrightly certain gentler emotions. This, of course, does not mean that he cannot be firm and demanding as the situation warrants. But, through the integration of both firmer and gentler emotions, a man's total relationships are being enriched.

The new role of the modern husband permits him to be a team worker with his wife. In fact, the whole family, including the children, is a team. The husband is no longer the captain of a ship, shouting commands to a subservient crew. He is, rather, one among equals, as the family cooperatively plans and works toward certain goals. The "captain" concept of leadership is passé in the modern world of business as well. The boss no longer commands, but rather is expected to be versed in interpersonal relationships, thus enabling him to *elicit* cooperation. The team worker husband and father provides greater opportunity for various members of the family to achieve their greatest potential as individuals. In fact, there is an appreciation of individual differences among family members.

Briefly, the new role of a man permits a broader range of experiences and relationships, especially with his family. He is also learning that he can express his masculinity through emotions formerly reserved for women. This is enriching his emotional life. Of course, as modern men are learning to do this, certain conflicts are inevitable as they learn what it is to be a man in the twentieth century. Many will experience the conflicts described in the chapter on demasculinized men. But we must not let their problems deflect our attention from the fact that most husbands and fathers are making adequate adjustments toward discovering more meaningful channels of expressing their masculinity.

THE NEW STATUS OF WOMEN

"To be a woman is something so strange, so confused, so complicated, that only a woman could put up with it." [8] These words by Søren Kierkegaard attempt to express some of the difficulties confronted in being a woman. One of the most articulate and bitterest statements in recent times about the predicament of women was made by Simone de Beauvoir in her book *The Second Sex*. Woman, the second sex, must always stand in the shadow of her husband, who demands that she be all his, but does not respond in kind. A member of the second sex must be subservient to her husband even though she herself is a talented and competent person in her own right.

This description of woman's dilemma is in the state of transition and is becoming outmoded. To be sure, American women still confront many of the problems to which *The Second Sex* addresses itself, a fact that made my chapter " The Unfulfilled Wife " necessary. But there is as much comparison between many of the competent modern wives and their male-dominated sisters of another era as there is between a new Cadillac and a Model T Ford. Ackerman says that the contemporary image of the modern husband and father is of a *man* who stands in the shadow. He, not his wife, is now the forgotten person.[9] The modern wife has achieved a new status that is opening to her doors of opportunity previously pad-locked and stamped " Men Only! " She is certainly going through a struggle learning to integrate these newfound opportunities much as minority groups go through periods of confusion upon gaining new freedoms. Many of the conflicts of women are simply healthy " growing pains " as they throw off outmoded roles and endeavor to discover more adequate ones.

Evidences of the healthy aspects of the new status of women abound. Three of these are outstanding.

First, educational opportunities for women are continuously expanding. In fact, present indications are that the current woman has more education than the average man: ten years, compared to nine for men.[10] The idea that education spent on women is largely wasted is passing. Education is a frightening weapon to those who stand to gain by another's ignorance. Perhaps this is one reason why advanced education for women was so vigorously opposed. This fear is very well stated in a Brahmin saying: " Educate a woman and you put a knife into the hands of a monkey." [11]

American women have become educated and they are using this " knife " to carve out new roles for themselves in an industrialized society. They are learning to use their minds, and many are able to more than hold their own ground with men whether in discussions or in work opportunities.

At the present time, about 9 percent more girls are graduating from high school than boys. But there are about twice as many men as women in college. Thus higher education is still something of a man's province. Many people may not realize it but the first public-supported high school for girls was opened a little more than a hundred years ago, 1848, in Philadelphia. [12]

One of the encouraging new trends in education for women indicates that they are continuing their education after years of marriage and rearing a family. This provides a " second chance " for the woman who married before she completed her college education or who wants to brush up on certain studies prior to building a new career for herself, now that her children are less dependent on her. But this is not always easy, since, as Esther Rauschenbush observes, some universities are reluctant to admit a middle-aged woman with no college work or whose previous college credits are now two decades old. [13]

Dr. Carolyn G. Heilbrun argues that a girl is best equipped to do college work when she is in her thirties, since at twenty she is likely to be striving " as much for the acquisition of a bachelor as for a bachelor's degree." [14] Several universities have developed programs specifically geared to the needs of these women who are now continuing their education in preparation for the next " chapter " in their lives. In a society such as ours, which can utilize all the trained talents available, this seems to offer new possibilities in conserving manpower that would otherwise be lost. That women are able to pursue advanced education is indicative of their new status in the society.

A second indication of the new and elevated status of women in modern society is their broadened work opportunities. In fact, women are now employed in all but two or three occupational classifications listed by the Census Bureau.[15] This is an astounding change in the status of women, especially when one remembers that a few score years ago, women, for the most part, were required by public opinion to stay at home or, at best, work in some type of domestic employment outside the home.

One advantage enjoyed by the modern wife is that she can elect to work at home or outside the home. Her predecessors had no such choice. Neither does her husband, who has to work to support the family. However, a study by Lamar Empey of nearly 2,400 high school and college students found that the great majority of girls still prefer marriage to a career. Eight out of ten college girls express such a preference.[16] But it is not really necessary to choose either marriage or a career. The number of married women in the professions and business is evidence of this.

Work outside the home is made possible by several changes. One of these is that the modern wife has been relieved of much of the drudgery of housekeeping. For example, washing now requires no more than the few minutes necessary to put clothes into the automatic washer. It was nearly an all-day project for grandmother, for she had to pump the water from the well, build a fire to heat the water in a cast-iron pot, scrub the clothing on a washboard, and then hang them out to dry. Many girls now growing up hardly know what a clothespin looks like! The end result is that the wife can do her housework in less time. This mechanization of the home, however, has increased her dissatisfaction there, thus creating an urge in her to find meaningful activity outside.

Another factor that enables the wife to work is her greater education or job training, which equips her for working outside the home. Beyond the changes that are taking place within the home and within women, a change has also been taking place in the attitudes of the society toward working women. This removing of the stigma attached to women working has encouraged increasing numbers of them to move into the labor force. Approximately one third of the labor force is now women. As noted in the chapter " Unfulfilled Women," there is much less acceptance for mothers of small children working. But even this is likely to change as more adequate mother-substitute care for small children is provided in the society, and as we know more surely what the impact of this is on the children.

Now it may very well be asked why the broadening of work opportunities for women is necessarily a desirable feature. It is a positive sign simply because it means that one half of the adult population of our society has the opportunity to achieve whatever self-fulfillment comes through meaningful activity in the larger world.

The new status of women affords greater opportunities for personal development. Women of the past generations had little opportunity to develop more than the maternal and domestic aspects of their personalities. This is changing. Whatever personal growth, whatever satisfactions are afforded through education, through gainful employment, through contacts in the broader community — these are available to an increasing number of American women.

This chance for personal development through opportunities in the larger community is especially important for the single woman. The old maid aunt was often an object more of pity than of admiration. Her work choices were limited and she often had to live with relatives. The modern " bachelor girl " is permitted by society to pursue most types of work and live as rich and fulfilling a life as she is capable of and desires to achieve. In fact, the freedom and abandon with which she lives may on occasion be envied by her married sisters.

The modern woman is achieving equality with men. There is certainly a sense in which this is true. But Max Lerner seems to have come closer to the truth in reading beneath the battle cries of feminists of an earlier day. He feels that woman's struggle with man has not been so much for *equality* as for *identification.* " The bobbed hair," he says, " the latchkey of her own, the cigarette, the cocktail, the ballot, the pay envelope, proved to be symbols of a quest not so much for equality as for identity." [17] This need for a sense of identity, for a sense of personhood, has been an underlying motivation in the efforts of women to achieve certain goals. But this sense of identity moves deeper than simply a feeling of acceptance as a person by men. It also includes discovering her identity *as a woman* in the mid-twentieth century. She cannot do this by adhering to feminism, for, as Nelson Foote observes, the feminist was in reality more masculine in that she rejected conventional femininity and took men for her model.[18] Again, Max Lerner makes sense by saying, " If she is to discover her identity, she must start by basing her belief in herself on her womanliness rather than on the movement for feminism." [19]

There is another word that seems to characterize the efforts of women: freedom. They have sought and made great progress in being granted the same personal freedom experienced by men: freedom to have a say in family decisions; freedom to share in local, state, and national affairs; freedom to develop responsibly their lives as seem appropriate; freedom to contribute to the family income as well as to its expenditures. Christian women especially have good reason to seek freedom, for the message of Christ is, " You will know the truth and the truth will make you free " (John 8:32). Some interpret this in a strict spiritual sense as free from sin, but this seems arbitrary. Who can evade the message of Paul, who asserts, " There is neither Jew nor Greek, there is neither slave nor free, there is neither male nor female; for you are all one in Christ Jesus " (Gal. 3:28). Some of the arbitrary distinctions between men and women in the light of this verse seem highly questionable. Nonetheless, the church historian, Latourette, says that Christianity was responsible for elevating the status both of women and of children in the early centuries.[20]

In concluding this section on the new status of women, it is appropriate to note that some feel that the status of women in the modern church does not seem to have kept pace with that in the secular world.[21] It is encouraging to note, however, that an increasing number of women are seeing the challenge of church vocations and are training for these positions. They are largely involved in music and religious education. Few churches seem ready to accept a " Reverend Mrs." But if some denominations continue to have trouble recruiting sufficient men for pastoral positions, this is one alternative they face — to recruit women.

Having discussed some aspects of the new status of women, we have said in effect that women have opening to them vast new vistas for personal development and growth. The last battle has not yet been fought, however. Both men and women are having difficulty learning to live with this new type of woman. But it is worth the effort.

THE NEW STATUS OF CHILDREN

One of the most apparent changes in the American culture has to do with the new status of children. Few values rank higher in our hierarchy of values than children. A salesman who can demonstrate that his product will help the children has just about sold it. Churches feel the same way. Many a pastor will gladly tell of his youth program. He may even have a full-time youth worker. By contrast, he will probably say nothing of what he is doing for the older people in the church because our society places a low valuation on age.

Children from the era when they were to be seen and not heard would probably think they were in paradise were they to look in on a modern home. They would see children with expensive toys, freedom to express opinions contrary to those

of their elders, sizable allowances, few chores, and being chauf-
feured around by their parents as if they were the governor.
There are those who feel this has gone too far. Some say we
live in a child monarchy. Too often this is true. Gibson Winter
says child rule is inevitable when the father abdicates his role
and the mother refuses to be the center of family life.[22] Children that grow up under circumstances where they " call the
plays " too frequently become frustrated, self-centered, rebel-
lious adults. Americans have moved from one extreme of
" *Spare* the rod and spoil the child " to " *Use* the rod and spoil
the child."

All is not hopeless. Parents are moderating. Perceptive parents now know that a child, in order to develop emotional
health, needs both firmness and gentleness. He needs discipline, meted out with firmness and consistency, warmth and
love.

It would be easy to dwell on the unhealthy aspects of the
relationship with our children. But there are at least three
constructive facets of the new status of children.

First, there is a new concern for the rights of children. Until
modern times the rights of children were few. Children were
often handled by the courts as if they were adults. Numerous
accounts are on record of children being executed for relatively minor offenses. With the rise of industrialization, children were put to work for long hours in factories where light
was at a minimum, safety unthought of, and education an
impossibility. Slowly but surely, child-labor laws were enacted
to limit or prevent such wanton exploitation.

One of the prime movers fostering national concern for the
rights of children have been the several White House conferences on children. The first of these conferences was called by
President Theodore Roosevelt in 1909. Since 1930 the President has called another each decade. Katherine Oettinger,
chief of The Children's Bureau of the Department of Health,
Education and Welfare, says it is significant that the United
States is the first nation in the world to establish (in 1912)

such a bureau, whose sole concern is the welfare of children.[23]

Beyond concern for a child's rights to an education, physical health, and protection from exploitation, our generation is concerned about their social and psychological rights. For example, the Children's Charter adopted by President Hoover's White House Conference in 1930 begins by asserting that it is the right of every child to have " understanding and the guarding of his personality as his most precious rights." [24] We believe a child has a right to certain experiences that foster social skills and happiness. The child has a right to certain opinions of his own and most parents will let a child express opinions for which, a generation ago, he would have gotten a sound thrashing. Some also feel that a child has a right to get angry at the parent, even as the parent gets angry with the child.

One of the earliest concerns for the rights of children is expressed in the Bible when Paul admonishes, " Fathers, do not provoke your children to anger " (Eph. 6:4). He is not simply urging parents not to frustrate and enrage their children. This is inevitable if they are good parents. I take this to mean that parents ought not to relate to their children in such a manner that the children grow up "mad at the world." Pastors and counselors regularly see adults who are angry at the whole world usually because their right to a happy, stable home as children was denied.

These rights are related to the encouragement for the child to develop his own personality, which will be discussed in more detail below.

A second facet of this new status of children is that the birth of children can now be a matter of choice. The motto of the Planned Parenthood Association, " Every child a wanted child," expresses this idea very well. It has not always been so. Children for countless centuries have too often been the incidental by-product of adult pleasure. With the development of effective contraceptive devices and the spread of such information, it is possible for families to have children when they want them. (This, of course, does not include those cir-

cumstances where couples have difficulty initiating pregnancy.)
This does not mean there are no longer "accidents," but it
does mean that a child is more likely to be born now because
his presence is desired by the parents. They want someone to
love, to complete themselves.

The modern child is more likely to be desired for his own
sake. Children were economic assets when families lived on
farms. They made good farmhands. In fact, children in urban
life are distinct economic liabilities. The reasons motivating
parents to have children are profound and moving. Some persons have supposed that if the human sexual urge were to
cease, people would cease to have children. Others doubt it.
Adults would continue to have children partly because they
need the experience of cuddling an infant, of teaching and
training a child, of sharing the adventure of seeing him grow
into adulthood, and of knowing that through it all they are
having a profound, creative, enriching experience. Children
are made to love. They can soak it up by the gallon. Every
child has the right to be born into a home where he can be
so loved.

A third facet of this new status of children is that there is
now a recognition of individual differences and potentialities
in children. Perceptive parents are quick to note how different
each of their children are. One is more placid, the other more
active; one outgoing, the other retiring. One child may be
good at abstract thinking, whereas another likes to work with
his hands. The reasons why these differences exist are not
clear. The most usual answer attributes them to environment.
But some authorities are now saying that heredity plays a more
important role in one's temperament and pace of life than we
have been aware.[25]

Modern parents are likely to take into account these differences and encourage each child to develop the healthy tendencies of his own personality. The schools do likewise. The
rigid curriculum of earlier schools sometimes did as much
damage as good to a child. Children are now often encouraged

to move at their own pace and develop their own individual interests.

The emerging democratic home encourages the various members of the family to develop their own potentialities. The children are encouraged to use their minds, and express their own opinions and feelings. The parents in these homes usually consult the children on family policies and explain family regulations to the child in a rational way. One study of children who were reared in democratic homes found three things. First, these children tended to demonstrate a more active, socially outgoing type of behavior. They were more expressive of both friendly and hostile feelings. Secondly, the children usually occupied favored positions in their groups. Thirdly, these children usually rated high on activities that required creativity and intellectual curiosity.[26] All these qualities are in harmony with the high valuation placed by many parents on making use of a child's individual differences.

One of the most pathetic experiences is to see a parent trying to force a child into a role that is out of keeping with his personality or into an activity in which he has no interest. The father who tries to make a football hero out of his son who cannot tolerate such competition will be thoroughly frustrated himself and might cause his son to develop a feeling that he is unmanly. The same boy, on the other hand, may thoroughly enjoy the thrill of competing with the football player for an A in biology.

If parents will listen closely to their children, if they will keep their " antenna " up, they can avoid many problems. For " out of the mouths of babes " often come profound truths. One of the counselor's most difficult tasks in dealing with parent-child difficulties is getting the parent to hear the child out. One father reported that this truth did not come to him until one day, during a disagreement between the two of them, his six-year-old son said, " But, Daddy, you're not listening to me." At first, he thought the boy impudent. Then it struck him that he really was not listening. He had his mind already made up as to what his son was trying to say. He was wrong. The problem was solved in short order.

The new status of children is to be desired. In its healthiest manifestations it means that they are viewed as persons in their own rights. They are not little adults. One therefore cannot expect adult behavior of them. But neither are they incapable of *any* understanding and responsibility if properly approached. At times, they frustrate parents beyond their last outpost of patience. This is part of parent and child learning to live together. It is part of a child's learning how to be a child. But parents should not be too harsh on themselves, for they are learning how to be parents. One father reports that on occasion when his first child, a son, was small he would do something and immediately know he had wronged the child. He would then pick up the crying son — they have a way of knowing when a parent is " off base " — and say to him: " Son, Daddy is sorry; he didn't mean to do that. But, you see, I've never been a Daddy before and I'm having to learn how — just like you're having to learn how to be a little boy." This father has a daughter now. He is still saying the same thing, because he has never been the father of a little girl.

14

STRENGTHENED MARRIAGE CONCEPTS

THE TERMS in which Americans conceive marriage have changed
— in bases, goals, and satisfactions. Some bemoan this fact,
saying it has contributed to increased marital unhappiness and
family discord. This argument can rally much support. But all
aspects of the new terms in which marriage is conceived are
not negative. This chapter will discuss two of these: marriage
as a companionship, and certain constructive aspects of romantic love. These, it is felt, are part of the strengths of modern marriage.

MARRIAGE AS A COMPANIONSHIP

For some time, marriage has been moving away from an institutional toward a companionship basis. This is the basic
idea contained in Burgess and Locke's book *The Family: From
Institution to Companionship*. Their oft-quoted preface succinctly states their thesis:

In the past the important factors unifying the [institutional]
family have been external, formal, and authoritarian, as the
law, the mores, public opinion, tradition, the authority of the
family head, rigid discipline, and elaborate ritual. At present,
in the new emerging form of the companionship family, its
unity inheres less in community pressures and more and more

in such interpersonal relations as the mutual affection, the sympathetic understanding, and the comradeship of its members.[1]

This is another way of saying that in the past, marriage has been primarily a contract between two people in which the functions of the family — economic, reproductive, protective — along with concerns of the community were the most significant cohesive factors. The more personal relationships between husband and wife were of lesser significance.

This shift from external unifying factors to more subjective ones was inevitable with the spread of industrialization and the greater freedom of women. With the transfer of functions formerly performed by the home to agencies outside the home, a new "mortar" to unify family members was necessary. Woman's greater freedom was accompanied by more permissive public opinion and economic independence. She therefore no longer *had* to stay with her husband. Though these older binding forces are by no means extinct, they no longer carry the same impact they once did. In their place is emerging a concept of marriage that is based on more personal qualities. This new type of family has been variously termed companionship, democratic, equalitarian, and colleague. Perhaps each term has a little different emphasis, but they generally refer to the same type of family. For the sake of uniformity, the term "companionship" is used here.

What are the qualities of this new family? As already indicated, its basic hallmark is an inner cohesion based on love rather than legal and community compulsion. Modern couples are, for the most part, of the opinion that the only marriage worth contracting or preserving is one based on free choice, willing loyalty, and mutual respect. It is a partnership. They expect and demand a sense of sharing and participation in each other's life. Members of the family are equal, though performing different roles. There is an expectation that decisions involving the whole family will be arrived at by the whole family, including the children. Each member participates in the decision at the level of his own ability. Members of the companionship family are encouraged to develop their own interests and potentialities.

Couples who view marriage as a companionship put emphasis on doing things together, upon talking with each other, on planning together, on equalizing the responsibility for meeting the needs of the family, and on confiding in each other. However, an interesting aspect of confiding in one's husband is revealed in the research of Blood and Wolfe. They found that, in general, the longer a couple lived together, the more infrequently a wife turned to her husband with her troubles. That was done most in the honeymoon period.[2] They also found that the greater the husband's income, the more likely a wife was to confide in her husband about her problems. But beyond a ten-thousand-dollars-a-year income there is a steady decline of confiding.[3] Apparently these husbands are too busy making money to listen. Among other things, this suggests that the companionate marriage is, to a large degree, a middle-class phenomenon, as represented by the low percentage of uneducated wives who share troubles with their husbands. The fact that confiding declines as couples grow older suggests the emergence of other sources of satisfaction in the marriage.

Companionship as a basis for marriage is not new. Henlee Barnette notes that the Book of Genesis gives companionship as one reason for the creation of marriage.[4] " It is not good that . . . man should be alone," said the Creator. John Calvin asserted that the companionship aspect between husband and wife took precedence over the sexual one.[5] But if the concept of companionship is not new, the *emphasis* is. It has been elevated to a position of paramount importance. One of the most frequent complaints voiced to pastors, counselors, and others by unhappy mates is not necessarily that the husband or wife is irresponsible or abusive but simply that the mate will not relate in such a way as to communicate a sense of companionship, of sharing in the other's life. Many of the "mental cruelty" divorces involve nothing more than the absence of this sense of companionship.

All this means that greater responsibilities have been placed upon marriage. Not only is marriage to fill certain former economic, reproductive, and protective functions, but in addition it is to provide the sense of relatedness and community that humans need. As was noted in an earlier chapter, many of these needs were formerly met in the larger community by a sense of belonging to people around them. But American families are isolated and lonely. They have been thrown more and more onto one another for the satisfaction of these psychic needs. Perhaps Max Lerner is right when he says that no people in the world make greater demands upon marriage than Americans.[6]

The emphasis on marriage as a companionship rather than an institution, upon internal rather than external cohesion, means that many unhappy marriages now dissolve rather than "stick it out, regardless." This is rightly deplored by many family specialists, since a couple may be prone to "abandon ship" at the first sign of discontent rather than to stay, determining to resolve their difficulties. It is this determination to make the relationship work, Alfred Kinsey says, which makes the difference between the success and failure of many a marriage.[7] It also means that the marital vow to maintain the marriage "for better or worse, . . . till death do us part," has become more of a formality than a binding promise between the individual and God. That is, in practice, marriage has become an agreement between two people rather than an agreement between the two people and God.

Although couples with companionate marriages may tend to consider divorce too quickly when conflict arises, there is a strength emerging out of the confusion. These couples also seem to have a greater willingness to attempt reconciliation in cases of infidelity. Where marriages still have a heavy carry-over of institutional ideals, a mate may feel under *obligation* to dissolve the marriage in such instances, especially where the wife is the one who has "gone wrong." Furthermore, in localities where institutional concepts prevail, there may be community pressure for divorce. But the companionate marriage is better equipped to absorb such blows, being more flexible, and the couple, with repentance and forgiveness, can begin work at restructuring their relationship.

The two paragraphs above outline certain undesirable aspects of the companionate marriage: the tendencies to hasty divorce and neglect of the religious facet of marriage. But all is not despair. The institutional concept of marriage was ideally suited to the world in which it existed. However, the conditions which held that marriage together have changed. Public opinion now nods in agreement for many divorces. Greater freedom for women and broader work opportunities mean they are no longer financially dependent upon their husbands. The legal structure of the society makes divorce easier now than it was formerly. If these forces do not bind a couple together, then something else must. The quality of interpersonal relationships — affection, understanding, sharing — seems to have filled a void. This modern ideal of inner cohesion, many feel, is an improvement over the older ideal of staying in the marriage regardless of how miserable one becomes. It offers greater potential for the development of personal fulfillment and happiness. However, in the transitional period between the institutional type of marriage and the time when the companionate marriage is fully achieved, the instability of family life is pronounced. But, as Ernest Burgess notes, family life will doubtless stabilize once the transition is made.[8]

Presently, the companionate marriage seems to offer the greatest potential for marital happiness. Some research indicates that couples in our society who report the highest percentage of happiness are those where the husband and wife participate in family decisions equally. In one sample of 2,596 couples, Paul Popenoe found that only 47 percent of the marriages were rated happy where the woman was head of the house. When the man was believed to be the head of the house, 61 percent were rated happy. But where both husband and wife exercised equal control of the family, 87 percent were rated happy.[9] Although Dr. Popenoe's sample was comprised mainly of the educated middle class, his study raises interesting questions about other groups.

What about the future of the companionate marriage? Helen Ingersoll predicts that the movement toward this type of marriage will continue to grow.[10] Not only will this type of marriage grow, but it offers unusual opportunity for growth for the husband and wife. This is especially true of the wife. This type of marriage affords her greater opportunities to utilize her knowledge, skills, and education than the patriarchal marriage, for, in companionate marriages, it is expected that each member contribute of himself to the relationship. Although some wives still " play dumb," there is less reason for them to do so in a companionate marriage. This concept of marriage seems to imply continued personal growth on the part of both partners.

In the future, companionate marriages will also become increasingly stable as the society moves beyond the present transitional period. It has already been indicated above that this type of marriage seems to offer more in the way of possibilities for fulfillment and happiness in an industrialized world than any other type yet conceived. Perhaps, as the companionate marriage comes more clearly into focus, couples will also discover new strength in ancient truths about marriage being more than a private contract between two individuals — it also involves their relationship to God.

ASPECTS OF ROMANTIC LOVE

The only socially approved reason for marriage in our society is love. It would be considered almost immoral to marry because " he has money," or, " her father is president of the company," or because " she is educated." Love alone is acceptable. But love is such a nebulous term. To some, love is a sober-minded, intellectual response. To others, it is a starry-eyed emotion which wafts one away to Elysian fields to sip the nectar of the lotus eternally in the presence of the beloved. It is this latter type which draws the fire of family specialists who attribute to this romantic love much of the marital unhappiness experienced in our society.

In spite of those who berate romantic love, this section proposes to defend it — at least some of its aspects. Romantic love cannot be all wrong. Even a stopped clock is right twice a day! Ever since Ernest Burgess wrote of the deleterious effects of romantic love in 1926, various authorities and authors have attacked it. Apparently no one likes romance but the people. And there is ample evidence that they do like it, since a large percentage of songs, movies, and advertisements use romance as an appeal. Though few defend it, apparently every healthy young person and adult is now in the state of, or has enjoyed and been enriched by, romantic love. The only serious attempts, to my knowledge, to defend romance have been made by Clark Elzey in his book *Keeping Romance in Your Marriage,* and by Thomas Knight in an article.[11] In his article, Knight makes a comparative analysis of an opponent of romance, Denis De Rougement, and the Danish existentialist, Søren Kierkegaard, who, with some qualifications, was an exponent of romance.

Before we proceed further, perhaps some definition should be made of romantic love. It is usually depicted as being basically an irrational, unrealistic, idealistic, reality-distorting process strongly tinged with sexual attraction. Max Lerner says it is characterized by at least two elements.[12] The first is a conviction of uniqueness as represented in the belief, "You are the only one for me in the whole world." There is a "right" person somewhere who will appear in due time, perhaps "across a crowded room." The second element involves submission to fate. This overpowering sense of fate leads the couple to the conclusion, "This thing is bigger than both of us."[12] James Peterson says there is a third element, an optimistic attitude about the future.[13] That is, if one marries his predestined mate, then that love can surmount all barriers they might encounter in the future.

That this unrealistic, reality-distorting love is at the root of much marital discord is incontestable. Disillusionment seems to be especially characteristic of the areas of personal freedom, marital roles, having children, in-law relationships, values on neatness, values on savings and money, and attitudes toward divorce. Furthermore, men are more disillusioned by sex after marriage than women.[14]

Granting all of this, are there not some positive aspects of this love which idealizes the mate? Is not some idealization desirable? If romantic love creates an illusion, are not some illusions necessary to healthy living? I believe the answer to all these questions is yes.

Perhaps it would be well to note that romance is nothing new, though its *emphasis* in modern life is new. The Song of Solomon is a beautiful, warm work of art in which the writer attempts to express his love for his beloved. A few lines are illustrative:

> Set me as a seal upon your heart,
>   as a seal upon your arm;
> For love is strong as death,
>   jealousy is cruel as the grave.
> Its flashes are flashes of fire,
>   a most vehement flame.
> Many waters cannot quench love,
>   neither can floods drown it.
> If a man offered for love
>   all the wealth of his house,
>   it would be utterly scorned.
>
> — S. of Sol. 8:6-7 (RSV)

The sentiment expressed in this ancient Hebrew poem is as current as next month's popular hit, though phrased more beautifully and eloquently. Thus, the romantic concept of burning desire to be with the loved one, of an awareness of the other's physical desirability (as also revealed in The Song of Solomon), of an idealization of the other, are not new. Others have loved as deeply, as passionately, as warmly, as purely as any twentieth-century man and woman.

Inherent in romantic love is an awareness of the beloved as a member of the opposite sex. This may be as subtle and innocent as the fact that a boy finds drinking a soda with a girl more enjoyable than drinking one with a fellow. It may be more pronounced in that the other provokes specific sexual urges. Is this to be decried? Family counselors see in graphic situations the misery and frustration of men and women who are unable to respond with this spark of romance, of finding the mate physically desirable even though they are good " friends." Henry Bowman underlines the significance of this love in these words:

Romantic love, the love into which we fall, the love that prefaces and carries over into marriage, is distinguished from other types of love — filial, parental, brotherly — by the fact that it grows out of an awareness of and response to sex differences. Its focus is a person of opposite sex who is considered an outlet for sexual urges, stimulator of sexual responses, and an objective of marital aspirations.[15]

That is, romantic love should be only the beginning of a more profound love, if a couple continue their relationship. One of its basic components, a physical attraction, does not cease, but " carries over into marriage," to use Dr. Bowman's words. If this " spark " fails, the marriage may very well have been dealt a death blow. And this spark is a part of romantic love.

Romantic love is also criticized because of the fantasy it builds up around the love object, shrouding its true nature. Willard Waller states it in these words:

In romantic love one builds up an almost completely unreal picture of a person which he calls by the same name as the real person, and vainly imagines to be like that person, but in fact the only authentic thing in the picture is the emotion which one feels toward it.[16]

Of course, Dr. Waller is right if this is the predominant feature of a couple's relationship. But perhaps some fantasy about the mate characterizes most successful marriages.

Dr. O. J. Hodges is of the opinion that a certain degree of fantasy or idealization is important in marriage, but he distinguishes between two types of fantasy, " weaned " and " unweaned." [17] An unweaned fantasy, he says, is a product of wish fulfillment without insight. It is unweaned in that it tends to be compulsive and obsessive. It has not dealt with reality. On the other hand, a weaned fantasy maintains its wish-fulfilling function, but has worked out a compromise between the wish and reality. Now what does this have to do with romance in marriage? Just this. In the initial phases of a courtship, a romantic attraction develops. At this stage the girl feels: " This is the guy of my dreams. He's handsome, fun to be with, and fills my dreams at all points. He's all that I want." If she marries at this point, trouble lurks ahead. She has failed as yet to come to grips with the reality that he is *not* all that she wants. No one is. If reality does press in upon her, and a flaw becomes apparent, she may deny its existence rather than face it. The unweaned aspect of her fantasy may also cause her to try to remake her husband into the likeness of her mental image of him. She may spend hours trying to convince her friends that he is all she thinks he is. The real danger lies in the time when her illusions are ripped away. For instance, she may catch him in a lie. Disillusionment ensues. Within, she feels: " I've been deceived! I never though he was capable of this kind of thing." She then " falls out of love," which means that whatever positive illusions she had about him are withdrawn.

How might another girl handle this situation? She likely would go through the same " man of my dreams " process.

At some point in the relationship she comes to grips with the reality that her man is not some god on a pedestal. Her mental perception of him bears a reasonable resemblance to the person he really is. Upon catching him in the lie, she would doubtless be angry or hurt, but she would recover and continue to love him. Within herself, she would feel: " You're not the great guy I thought you were, but I still think you are wonderful. You are still my dream guy even though you don't fill my dream at all points." She still has illusions about him, but they have come to grips with reality. She is willing to accept him for what he is; and equally important, she will let others accept him for himself. There are cases when a mate may not come to view the other realistically until, through marriage counseling, this function is developed.

Certain illusions in life are necessary. Willard Waller mentions these when discussing what he calls constructive and destructive quarrels.[18] In a destructive quarrel, he says, each attacks certain illusions that the other has about himself. A wife may know that she is not beautiful, but she does have certain illusions about herself that she is attractive and perceived as desirable by her husband. He strikes below the belt in a quarrel when he calls her a " big, fat slob " whom he finds repulsive. This destroys a necessary illusion that her husband finds her attractive. She hits below the belt when she calls him a " spineless little boy," because men need to feel that their wives see them as competent, masculine men.

One husband perceptively described this romantic illusion when he said he knew his balding head and growing girth had not improved his looks, but it made him feel good to hear his wife say that she still finds him handsome. At the same time, the years had not improved his " fifty-ish " wife's looks, but to him she was still an attractive person. He said he felt like a couple in a movie, *The Enchanted Cottage*, who physically were not handsome or beautiful, but so long as they remained in the cottage they took on a glow in which each saw the other as attractive. Or as another husband phrased it, " My wife is still the girl of my dreams though she is middle-aged and in menopause."

It is this spark of romance which casts a warm and necessary glow around one's mate. The glow may exist only in the mind of the perceiver but it provides an important element of the attraction two people have for each other. And in an age when external bonds binding marriages together have diminished, these internal bonds must be strengthened. Furthermore, the detachment and isolation of modern families means that individual members have fewer and fewer sources from which to draw their sense of importance and significance. This romantic aura tends to create a sense that at least someone perceives me as " somebody," as someone special and worth loving.

What has been asserted in this section is that it is true that much marital discord and disillusionment is caused by a romantic love that distorts reality. At the same time, it is important to recognize that certain aspects of romantic love are an important strength in modern marriage. When the romantic fantasies one has about the mate remain unweaned — have not come to grips with reality — conflict, possibly ending in divorce, will ensue. But where these fantasies deal with reality, the resultant weaned fantasy can strengthen a relationship. One may still project some of his illusions onto the other, but they are not totally unrealistic. These are necessary illusions.

Having said this, perhaps in emphasizing this positive aspect of romantic love, we have simply used different terminology to describe the same phenomena mentioned by other writers. For instance, Waller notes that romantic love must be transformed into a less impetuous, less sentimental affection called conjugal love. This results in what he calls a " working equilibrium." [19] Kierkegaard, a staunch defender of romance, found romance alone to be incomplete because it is founded on what he calls " hope." That is, it is preoccupied with the future. It must be complemented and transformed by " recollection " or a sense of the past.[20] Through a balancing of hope and recollection, the individual is able to relate himself concretely to the present. This is another way of saying that love comes to grips with reality.

If a weaned romantic love includes some illusionary aspects, perhaps this is to be desired. After all, love itself is an illusion, according to Theodor Reik, but as he says, it is the most important illusion of our lives.[21]

15

STRENGTH THROUGH LEISURE
AND FLEXIBILITY

THE MODERN FAMILY draws strength from unsuspecting sources. It may be from something as apparent as the new role of women or as subtle as the "do it yourself" movement. Increased leisure time and the flexibility of the contemporary family are two such strengths. However, many persons would never think of the urge to move as a family strength. It can be. At the same moment that they are strengths, leisure time and flexibility are part of the problems confronted by some people. Can man adapt to the increased leisure time afforded by mechanization, and more specifically, by automation? Can families adapt to the demands for flexibility by an industrialized society without falling into the pitfalls of rootlessness? The answer, I believe, is yes. Man has always adapted, though we have no way of knowing precisely what adaptations are necessary for the future. The genius of the human species is that it is highly adaptable. In his book, *Man Makes Himself,* Childe notes that, by all rights, man should have become extinct long ago. He is a slow, clumsy being and thus has no speed with which to escape danger; he has no sharp claws or teeth with which to fight; he has no thick hide or heavy fur to protect him from danger and the elements. He is protected only by his superior mind and the ability to use and adapt to his environment. This same ingenuity will help him to survive the problems incurred by two aspects of industrialization — leisure time and flexibility. Furthermore, he is finding in these the necessary strength to live in this new age.

INCREASED LEISURE TIME

Perhaps our society has the distinction of being the first one in the history of the world in which the great majority of the population has large amounts of leisure time available for use as desired. In primitive societies, life is preoccupied with the matter of providing the necessities of life, of keeping body and soul together. The harshness of life in frontier America left little time for leisure. Consequently, our forefathers placed work among their highest values. A frontier had to be tamed. Idle play was strictly forbidden by several legislatures in early America. The Assembly of Virginia in 1619 decreed that actors were not permitted in the territory " because we resolve to suffer no Idle persons in Virginia." [1] The tenth pin in modern bowling came into existence as an attempt to circumvent an early law forbidding ninepin bowling. The laws of another state forbade " the Game called Shuffle Board, in houses of Common Intertainment, whereby much precious time is spent unfruitfully." [2]

With the development and spread of the machine, it has become possible for fewer and fewer men to do more and more work. Personal industry has become less important. The workweek has dropped from an estimated eighty-four hours in 1800 to the present forty. Joseph Prendergast, executive director of the National Recreation Association (the very existence of which is an interesting commentary on our times), predicts a seven-hour workweek in another century.[3] One of the tasks confronting contemporary society is the utilization of these nonworking hours. They can be filled with boredom and meaninglessness. Couples with marital troubles find these hours a great strain — they have that much more time to be discontent with each other. Used constructively, these hours offer promise of new strengths, new dimensions of life.

Perhaps it would be well to define the term "leisure" at this point. This is not easy. To some, the term conjures up thoughts of an easy chair with an interesting book or a pleasant visit with old friends. However, as used here, the term refers to all time not devoted to one's basic livelihood. "Leisure" therefore includes recreation, puttering around the house, civic projects, certain church activities, and the like. There are persons who feel that this is too broad a definition. Sebastian de Grazia is of the opinion that the whole idea of Americans having much more leisure time than a century ago is largely a myth.[4] By the time one includes the part-time job, travel to and from work, work around the house, and other time-consuming activities, de Grazia asserts that the modern American husband is putting in nearly as many hours as great-grandfather did a hundred years ago. However, it seems to me there is a difference — most modern husbands can *choose* whether or not to take a second job, work around the house, or engage in other activities. The amount of work that he *has* to put in on the job has significantly been reduced from that of a century ago. It is the ability to choose how one spends his nonwork time that makes it leisure, but not necessarily recreation. The man of the house may choose to put new weather stripping around the door of his home, but he could also choose to sit in his easy chair.

In what ways does leisure time offer promise of strength to the modern family? Florence Kluckhohn notes the first among these when she observes that shorter working weeks and days are opening the way for an expansion of interests beyond the job. She continues by saying, "Herein lies one of the best hopes for a future integration of masculine and feminine interests and for total family interests as well."[5] One of the common complaints confronted by family counselors is that of a lack of jointly shared interests by husband and wife. Leisure time affords the opportunity for husbands, wives, and the children to develop these mutual interests. This is apparent in the realm of recreation, where the investment in a boat is a family affair and its use for water skiing, fishing, or simply cruising around is shared by the whole family. The integration of masculine and feminine interests is perhaps best seen in the concern of suburban husbands in the home. Their interest in painting the woodwork, planting shrubs, or building a recreation room in the unfinished basement is a source of deep satisfaction to those couples who enjoy working together on a common project. (This does have its dangers, since an occasional wife reports feeling that her husband is taking over the house.) A skin-diving husband and wife of my acquaintance have discovered a new interest in constructing a submarine in the basement from old auto hoods and various other parts salvaged from wrecked cars. Of course, leisure time does not necessarily mean the development of common interests. " It will depend," as Dr. Kluckhohn notes, " upon what interests are developed and whether they are of an order of creativity to produce significant joint satisfactions." [6]

The current generation of teen-agers are benefiting from their increased leisure time. In fact, they are sometimes referred to as the " leisured class." Compared to the young person living on a farm, they have few responsibilities. They are not exactly destitute either, since the nearly twenty million teen-agers in the United States have an estimated buying power of about ten billion dollars. One of the most important but perhaps least recognized ways in which they benefit from leisure time is that they are learning to draw their meaning in life in pursuits other than work. (Of course, leisure must be balanced with work and too many teen-agers are having trouble learning this truth.) Present and future generations are going to derive fewer and fewer satisfactions from their work. These satisfactions and meaning in life will of necessity have to come from what one does in the off-work hours. Many adults in the present generation know only how to work. Work is a way of life for them, and some think it is the *only* way of life. They do not know how to relax. Walter Kerr in *The Decline of Pleasure* asserts that the concept of work as being the only activity worthy of mature people is attributable to Jeremy Bentham and his philosophy of "utilitarianism." Neither do these people know how to derive significant meaning out of participation in community organizations or other group activities. Yet it is in recreation, community projects, and home activities that the next generation is going to have to draw much of its sustenance in life. Perhaps being in the " leisured class " now will help them to do this more constructively. Play consumes a part of one's leisure time, and Dr. Karl Menninger states that one of the traits found in psychiatric patients is " that they are deficient in the capacity to play, or at least to develop balanced recreational techniques." [7] He has found this ability to play significantly more highly developed among reasonably well adjusted persons.

Why has leisure become such an important topic in a growing body of serious literature? Of course, the most obvious reason is that the average American has several hours a day beyond those involved in a livelihood that must be spent doing something. If one includes the weekends, the total time available in a week to nonwork activities comes to seventy-two hours, not including eight hours sleep each night. (In saying this, I am keenly aware of the fact that " a woman's work is never done." But even they have time available.) Of course, much of this time is taken in necessary activities such as eating and getting to and from work. In view of the fact that so many people seem to " never have time for that," one wonders what does happen to these hours. The danger in all our busyness is that the hours become filled with empty activity, and meaninglessness ensues. Psychiatrists are increasingly aware of the fact that one of the basic problems confronted by many of their patients is a loss of a sense of purpose and meaning in life.[8] Much of this sense of purpose is supplied in doing something significant for one's livelihood, whether this be outside the home or work as a homemaker.

This brings us to the most important reason for the significance of leisure. People draw their meaning in life largely from their work. However, with the coming of the assembly line, automation, and plants employing thousands of people, it has become increasingly difficult to achieve that same sense of importance and achievement one formerly had. For instance, more autos are assembled in Kansas City than in any other city in the nation outside of Detroit. Many of these workers seek help with family and personal problems. The chief complaint made about their work is the sheer monotony of the assembly line and the depressing, devastating sense of being " just another cog in the machine." It is very difficult to feel a sense of achievement after working eight hours bolting on wheels. "You don't even have to think," remarked one of these "cogs." Even if at the end of a day he views the several hundred new cars in the vast parking lot, his contribution toward their being there is so small that he can hardly say, " Look at what I did! " The struggle between labor and management makes it difficult to feel a part of the company, for the workingman seems to see management as a powerful tyrant seeking to squeeze the last drop of sweat out of him for the least possible money. Hostility for this impersonal company is often thinly veiled. The wife of one of my acquaintances, eager to get into the working world, quit in three weeks, after she discovered that she sat on a line with fifty other girls and was constantly hounded by time-and-motion experts peering over her shoulders to determine whether she made any unnecessary movements. A farmer, upon hearing his son tell about life in a big factory, made this significant statement: " Well, I work long hours and don't make much money, but I'm my own boss, and at the end of the year when I hold an ear of corn in my hands, I know that I did it all myself — planted, plowed, and picked it." Few workers in an industrialized society can have this same sense of satisfaction that is derived from starting and finishing a product — without being pushed by a foreman or a schedule.

All this simply means that the most fertile field for finding a sense of purpose and meaning today and in the future lies

in what one does in his nonwork hours. Many find this sense
of meaning in working around the home, in recreational activities, in community service, or religious pursuits. This
problem is more acute for the so-called " workingman " than
for the professional man, since he is less likely to find a deep
satisfaction in his work. One of the differences between the
professional and nonprofessional person is that the former is
more likely to derive a sense of purpose and significance from
his work. The workingman is likely to be mainly interested
in the weekly check, and to get his real satisfactions elsewhere.[9] Perhaps this accounts for the fact that most of the
work in a church rides on the backs of the ordinary men on
the street. " My experience," observed one pastor, " is that
professional people usually don't make your best workers.
They're too busy elsewhere."

One of the healthiest new uses of leisure time is the " do it
yourself " movement. Several years ago, the U.S. Department
of Commerce estimated that " do it yourselfers " were spending six billion dollars a year on their various projects.[10] The
sale of home tools has become a multimillion-dollar business.
In 1954, twenty-four million dollars was spent on paint rollers
alone! [11]

The value of this type of work is that it provides an opportunity for a person to do something creative. There is a real
satisfaction in seeing a piece of cloth take shape into a dress
at the hands of Mrs. Housewife. This partly accounts for the
booming sale of sewing machines since World War II. And a
keen sense of satisfaction comes to the man of the house in
seeing space in the attic become an attractive room and to
know that he " created " the room himself out of his own
sweat, ingenuity — and blood. Modern man needs to work with
his hands. The machine age has given him a sense of in-
feriority, the sculptor Boris Blair asserts, by making his own
individual efforts seem insignificant. Blair continues:

One reason so many of us are despondent, worried, jittery is
that we are using our heads too much and our hands too little.

God gave us our hands to work with and when a man lets them grow useless and clumsy, he is trying to buck nature — and he pays with neuroses.[12]

Of course, everyone who has worked in the psychiatric ward of a hospital knows the truth of this statement, for they have seen patients work out their emotions in the occupational therapy shop by creating with clay, paper, paints, metal, and wood. Mr. Blair feels that modern man needs the sense of self-confidence and self-respect that " comes only from seeing something take complete form under his own hands." This is why the " do it yourself " movement is so important.

The use of leisure time provides one of the challenging areas for the modern church. There is the need for a development of a theology of leisure. Protestantism probably has a more clearly definied theology of work than of leisure. The Puritans, perhaps unfairly, get much of the credit for the emphasis on work and the depreciatory attitude toward leisure. However, Karl Menninger notes that this attitude has a more profound origin in a person's struggle to overcome the infantile tendency to act on the pleasure principle.[13] But God not only worked six days, he also rested on the seventh. Perhaps it is this seventh day that will provide a beginning point for a theology of leisure. Thus far the church has not been very systematic in pursuing the subject. In the main, churches have limited their concern with leisure to providing certain recreational activities for young people. A few churches now have recreational leaders on the staff (the recreationist is an emerging profession), though this responsibility is more often relegated to another staff member or the pastor.

At the present time, the church has difficulty asking significant questions in the realm of leisure and religion, much less providing answers. A provocative chapter, " Leisure and Religion," should provide " grist " for the pastor's mind and is found in Max Kaplan's book, *Leisure in America*. One of the difficult problems in this area is a precise definition of leisure. How does it differ from idleness or rest? How are leisure and worship related? What are the moral bases and functions of recreation? How is leisure related to the sanctification of time? Is there a hierarchy of values in the use of leisure time? Does the church have a responsibility to concern itself with leisure? How important is the freedom of the individual and the use of leisure time? How can the church integrate leisure time and a sense of purpose in life? These are some of the questions with which the church is confronted. As the answers to these are more clearly seen, personal and family life in the future will be increasingly strengthened.

GREATER FAMILY FLEXIBILITY

The auto trailer is an apt symbol of many modern American families. They are on the move. Because of the trailer, rentals have become a multimillion-dollar business. One out of every five families change residence each year, for which they pay an estimated one billion dollars in packing and moving costs.[14] Some families are so mobile that luxurious house trailers have come into existence, permitting a family to move with an hour's notice. In fact, Americans move so often that one observer asserts that the regular ten-year census is not sufficient in some localities to give the true picture of the dynamics of change in the intervening years.[15]

This ceaseless mobility of the family is a source of concern to many social scientists. They see in it the genesis of many of the problems that plague the modern family. Among other things, it contributes, they contend, to the breakdown of family and community ties, the kinds of ties that impart to a person a sense of belonging to, and responsibility for, his community. In the resulting rootlessness and isolation, a sense of meaninglessness, irresponsibility, and even lawlessness may overcome the individual. The social scientists are right. Mobility can and does contribute to such conditions in many instances. But the mobility of the American family has its positive aspects as well. It is the purpose of this section to defend the position that it is one of the strengths of the contemporary family. Of course, mobility is not the only expression of family flexibility, but it is perhaps the most dramatic demonstration of this trait of modern family life.

There is a sense in which American families have always been on the move. From the time the Pilgrim Fathers landed on the eastern coast, they began to push into the interior of the continent. The West, like a magnet, pulled adventurous and restless men toward it. The 1800's saw thousands of prairie schooners taking families to new opportunities, free land, and riches. They seldom found riches, but they always found hardship and sometimes death. Still, once the families became settled, they seemed to " stay put," and would hardly compare with the contemporary American who in a lifetime may move a dozen or more times.

The time is not too far past, especially in stable rural communities, when it was common for people to be born and die in the same locality. There is something very stabilizing to live in the same community where one was born, to plow the same soil you plowed as a kid, to walk the same roads as your fathers before you, to attend the same church you attended as a child, to marry a girl you knew from the time you were big enough to know what a girl was, and even to die in the same community in which you were born. Many Americans reflect with nostalgia to these years. But for the most part they are gone. They must take their place on the shelf of history along with the horse, buggy, and steam locomotive.

The new world of the contemporary generation seems to demand that families move. So they move. Like nomadic shepherds, they seem to be always in search of greener pastures. Although various studies indicate that this is a real problem to some families, there are people who seem to derive satisfaction from moving. The " itch to switch " is supplanting the seven-year itch. One of these wives reported that living the rest of her life in one community in the same house was utterly unthinkable. " About every four or five years," she said, " I want to see some new faces and enjoy a house with different room arrangements." Another wife is quoted as saying, " Any time the curtains get dirty, I'm ready to move." [16] Younger children probably adjust to new surroundings more easily than adults. However, it is families with adolescent children who usually seem to find moving the most difficult. The problem of developing new friends in a new community, of making their place in new high schools, can be a most difficult adjustment for the teen-agers. Their conflict focuses primarily on the sense of isolation experienced in the new setting because other kids already have formed their circle of friends. It is extremely important for the teen-ager to feel accepted as a part of a group.

Another problem with highly mobile families is being able to establish some type of roots in the community without getting the roots set too deeply. Otherwise, they experience a type of emotional shock upon moving. It is apparently possible for many people to develop this type of meaningful, but less profound, relationship with the community. The wife of one career military man reported that she and most other wives in her situation had simply accepted this type of nomadic life and that by now she ran into former friends on every new base to which her husband was assigned. This provides a type of continuity. Another wife compared developing friends with their highly mobile type of life to farming in Alaska. " With the short 'growing season' of these friendships," she said, " they have to mature in a hurry." Can friendships be hurried? Apparently they can. Although these " early maturing " relationships probably do not have the same deep values that are gained by developing friendships over a lifetime, they can be most meaningful. The culture in some circles dictates that deep relationships must develop over many years. For example, an older farmer in a stable rural community kept referring to himself as a " newcomer." Inquiry revealed that he had lived there more than ten years. Still he was a " junior " resident compared to those who had lived there a lifetime. On the other hand, in mobile urban areas there seems to be a feeling that it is not necessary to know one another for years before one is accepted into the " inner circle." This is fortunate, since modern life does not permit lifelong friendships for most residents.

Apart from migrant farm labor, persons in the upper occupational levels — professional and managerial men — are the most transient of any in our society.[17] As noted, these and " displaced persons " like them do not have the type of rootage developed by spending years in a community. But William Whyte, Jr., observes that their rootlessness is not of the old type. He refers to a nursery that advertises that its trees are transplanted several times before being sold, thus breaking up the large main roots and encouraging the growth of secondary roots close to the trunk.[18] This is an apt description of the transient American who is making an adequate adjustment to his type of life. Though he may long for deeper roots, he has learned to derive satisfaction out of these short-term relationships.

This ability to adapt with reasonable aplomb to new environments, to establish new relationships rather quickly, is to be desired in the mode of modern life. It is well to reminisce about the past, or expound about how things ought to be today, but the fact remains that families must live in the present under present conditions. The ability to adapt to rapid change is a part of the necessary " survival equipment " of the contemporary family. This may mean moving from one place to another or having the flexibility to adapt to changing communities, changing values, changing modes of transportation, changing styles of dress, and even changing religious concepts. (It was not too long ago that most ministers found the Biblical account of creation and the evolutional concept totally incompatible.) The inability to adapt to changes within oneself, the family, or the larger community, accounts for much of the maladjustment and emotional distress experienced by many people.

The new generation is learning to live with such change.

Although some do not possess this flexibility, others are discovering how to " roll with the punches " and make adequate adjustments to changes. They have long ago ceased to think only of their own community, and their horizons now include the international community. With the launching of the Russians' Sputnik in 1957, this generation's horizons were pushed even farther as they now attempt to adapt to a concept of limitless space. Before the nations have yet learned how to live together peaceably on earth, they are having to consider survival in space. One of the psychological problems of space existence is learning to live with the gnawing sense of total detachment and isolation from the earth. The prospects of life in space or a highly regimented life as depicted in Orwell's *1984* can be terrifying to the present generation. But the adjustment to that type of life will doubtless be made, even as man has learned to live in city dwellings instead of caves. Behavioral scientists, among others, are concerned with discovering ways of preventing as many " emotional wrecks " as possible in the constant transition in which society finds itself, for many are finding, and will continue to find, that such adaptation demands more flexibility than they possess.

PART IV

CONCLUSIONS FOR CHURCH AND FAMILY

16

THE CHURCH AND FAMILY NEEDS

HISTORICALLY, the church has been one of the most potent forces in the shaping of Western civilization. It continues to be so. But if its message is to continue to be relevant in a day when many a " voice in the wilderness " cries out to be heard, it must continuously reinterpret its proclamation. It is the purpose of this and the following chapter to pull together a few ideas dealt with or suggested in the preceding pages that are pertinent to the family, in the hope that they may help point the way for this continued relevancy. This is not to say that the church and the gospel it proclaims are outmoded. The redemptive love of God in Christ is still as pertinent and needed as in any previous generation. However, one of the major tasks of each generation is the reapplication or reinterpretation of this gospel to meet new manifestations of sin. To say to the average man on the street today, "You are lost! " will bring hardly more than a quizzical look, though it moved men to action under the preaching of Moody or Whitefield. Men are still lost, but their lostness is experienced in new guises such as the gnawing, pervasive sense of pointlessness and meaninglessness.

FAMILY AND CHURCH: COLLEAGUES

R. Lofton Hudson has a lecture entitled " The Church and Family: Competitors or Colleagues." The title is appealing because it touches on a question overtly or tacitly raised in the minds of many people. The multiplicity of demands by the many activities of a modern church can keep a conscientious family going *eight* days out of the week, causing some people, including denominational leaders, to express concern about the church pulling families apart! Of course, the basic thrust of the church-family relationship is not competitive, but complementary. Ernest Groves was correct in seeing the family and the Christian church as allies.[1] They are, indeed, colleagues.

That the home in which Jesus grew up made a profound impression upon him is incontestable in view of the way in which he used the family to demonstrate truths of the Kingdom. Relationships within the family became the terminology in which he expressed the relationships among his followers as brothers, as members of the household of God, and in which God is seen as Father. As Groves further notes:

> Nothing can so well uncover the importance of the family in the program of Christianity as this fact that Jesus needed to go to the vocabulary of family association for suggestive ideas that would have some hope of conveying the genius of his teaching to those who as co-workers were later to take over the task of a new spiritual crusade.[2]

Not only were family concepts used to convey truths of the household of God but Jesus also drew upon everyday family experiences to illustrate his message, the kind of experiences that would poignantly carry a message home to the hearer who could see a relationship between the real and the spiritual.

The church and family are colleagues, particularly in the religious education of children. For instance, poor parent-child relationships handicap, or negate, the religious education program for children. The home lays the foundation of basic religious concepts such as trust, love, and forgiveness. Astute religious educators are aware of the fact that a child whose life experiences have taught him that people are not to be trusted

because they will betray you, may also have difficulty learning
to trust God. Parents who make a practice of breaking promises to their child, or of betraying the child's confidence, may
not be aware of the fact that they are thereby making it difficult for the child to trust God. Stated more positively, a child
who learns to trust his earthly father finds it easier to trust
his Heavenly Father. And the child whose home fails to create
an atmosphere in which he learns to love may also have difficulty learning to love God. Children who grow up in homes
where forgiveness is absent, where parents continue to bring
up old wrongs, may have real difficulty believing, or at least
emotionally accepting the idea, that God forgives and forgets
one's sins. If the home has provided an atmosphere conducive
to learning to love, trust, and forgive, then the church has a
basis for teaching the child to trust and love God, and to
accept and understand his forgiveness. Of course, the home
and church work together in other ways in the religious education of children, but these examples are illustrative of this
partnership.

The above having been said, perhaps it is well to note that,
although the home exercises great influences in preparing the
child to accept God's message more readily, the child who
grows up in a home destitute of the qualities of love and trust
is not predestined to a life without God. Quite the contrary
is often true, since some of the most devout laymen and our
outstanding religious leaders come from such homes. To quote
one: " When I heard of God's love, it was really ' gospel ' to
me; the best good news I had ever heard! " However, this man
and others admit that the possibility of God's love reaching
into such homes in its greatest effectiveness is handicapped by
the emotionally deprived homes described above. And although they did not learn of love and trust from their earthly
father or mother, they frequently found in some Sunday school
teacher, pastor, or public-school teacher a meaningful parental
substitute to convey the message of these heavenly truths.

The church occupies a rather unique role in the life of the

family in that it is the only community organization working with the whole family. Other groups are concerned only with the children or with the adults, and have little if any interest in the others. The church ministers to all family members. Furthermore, the pastor is about the only professionally concerned person going into the modern home. Physicians and social workers are increasingly working from their offices. Neither do family counselors go into the homes. Certainly there are reasons why these professional people ask that the family come to them, the chief one being that they can see more people, but this is to be regretted in some ways because one visit in the home may be more revealing than several office visits. Fortunately, a pastor still has a ready entry into most homes by simply introducing himself with the almost magical words, " I am the Reverend Mr. Smith from the church down the street." (However, pastors in urban areas are finding that such unannounced knocks on the doors of their parishioners are not so welcomed as they once were. It is not that these parishioners do not wish to see their pastor, but as one lady said: " I do wish he [the pastor] had given me an hour's notice. I could have at least taken the rollers out of my hair! ")

The church and family also prove to be colleagues in a type of mutual support. The challenging study *Successful American Families*, by Zimmerman and Cervantes, discloses that successful families surround themselves with other successful families with whom they are friends. These families are similar to one another in several ways. They usually have a pronounced similarity of moral, ethical, and religious views. (Of course, this does not mean that successful families are necessarily deeply religious. Rather, successful families tend to surround themselves with other families of similar religious views, which may or may not be devout.) However, where the families are conscientious in their religious practice, a type of support of the church by the families is involved. At the same time, the church provides support and strength for the families.

Certainly the church provides maximal support for its families when it addresses itself to needs experienced by the families in its membership.

GEARING THE CHURCH TO MODERN FAMILY NEEDS

A perennial problem confronting the church is that of gearing its approach to meet the needs of the individuals and families that comprise its membership. There is reason to believe that the church is often out of touch with the needs of its people. As is sometimes said, " The church is still answering questions that people are no longer asking." J. C. Wynn cites one denominational survey in which pastors were asked to list the three most common areas of discord among married couples in their churches. The pastors concluded that drinking, sex difficulties, and religious disagreements were the real problems. The survey then asked the married couples themselves the same question. Their startling reply was that the real problems were money, in-laws, and child training.[3] Furthermore, Wynn feels that much of Protestantism is still geared to a nineteenth-century rural pattern of organization which throws it out of touch with the real needs of contemporary families.[4]

Many churches and denominations are aware of the need for updating their ministry of family education. One of the difficulties is that of determining precisely what are the real needs of families in the community. These needs are probably related to man's more basic needs for relatedness, meaning, involvement, creativity, challenge, rest, security, acceptance, and the meeting of his physical requirements. The translation of these into everyday life becomes the difficult part. Within the membership of each church are people with unfathomable anxieties and vast concerns over financial, physical, and emotional distress. Few churches are geared to do more than have the pastor make a call in these homes, which frequently leaves him feeling so frustrated and helpless that it is easier not to call on such families.

At times, some churches appear disinterested in the needs of people. An attendance officer with the public schools of a large city called on a pastor to ask that an effort be made to enlist a teen-age boy with a father in the late sixties in the church's youth program. The father was so totally out of touch with the needs of a fifteen-year-old boy that this, along with other factors, created a highly undesirable home atmosphere, and the boy seemed to be headed for trouble. Since this boy was from a lower-class home and lived in a low-rent housing project, the pastor candidly said, "Well, I'm not sure; you know we can't take too many of these people into our church or they will ruin it!" Nothing was done. A few weeks later a notice was received from the police department, indicating that the boy had been arrested for some crime. J. C. Wynn's observation on such situations is pertinent:

> The onetime compassion of the early Christians will not be recovered until the church as a whole becomes responsive to such needs, and until it sees in these adversities family-wide implications that need a healing touch of a committed fellowship.[5]

Perhaps one of the beginning places in gaining and maintaining contact with the needs of modern families is by establishing better lines of communication between the pulpit and pew. It is reported that in New Testament times members of the congregation would interrupt the preacher to ask questions or make observations. Preaching thus became a dialogue, an interaction between two people. If verbalized, the inner reactions of modern parishioners to statements made from the pulpit would probably be more instructive to the pastor than several seminary classes in homiletics, theology, and pastoral care. (This is not to suggest that the pastor be interrupted in the middle of his sermon next Sunday, though the reaction might be interesting!) It is not often that ministers and laymen have the opportunity to sit down together in a "secure" atmosphere in which each is free to express himself without fear of some type of recrimination. But the few instances in which it does take place prove to be refreshing experiences. One minister speaking to a group on communication between the pastor and his people proved to be so challenging that he was asked that night to return for a second such session. The people appeared to be hungry for this type of experience. However, this requires considerable maturity on the part of participants, since some ideas expressed can be most threatening to both pastors and parishioners.

In their sermons, pastors often unwittingly communicate the feeling that they are somehow not quite in touch with what "ordinary" people experience. Counselors occasionally ask people why they do not consult their pastor about their difficulties. An answer sometimes received is: " Oh, I couldn't talk with him. He is a nice person but I don't think he would really understand this type of thing." The pastor may know very well what the parishioner is experiencing, but has failed to communicate this sense of understanding to the person. Every pastor knows that his family life is basically the same as that of his parishioners. He knows loneliness, anger, doubts, guilt, and sexual feelings. He knows the feeling of having his daughter get a divorce, his son fall in with the wrong crowd, and his wife say, " I'll not take any of this one more day! " He meets the temptations of desire to acquire the status symbols, knows of the drive to succeed, and of the struggles within himself as he tries to scale the ladder to a social class foreign to what he has known. He knows the frustration of irritations arising out of getting the family ready for church on Sunday morning, the kind of thing that takes him out of the mood for preaching in the same way such irritations remove the spirit of worship from those who hear him. But his congregation may feel that he is somehow above all these problems.

The sensitive pastor, who, as the shepherd of his people, compassionately looks into the faces of his flock on Sunday morning and asks himself: " What message from God do these people need? What are their fears, their hopes, their burdens, their anxieties? " may find his preaching taking on new dimensions of relevancy and urgency.

THE CHURCH AND SOME SPECIFIC FAMILY NEEDS

The strengths and problems of the modern family have been the major thrust of the previous sections of this book. The purpose of the following pages is to reemphasize some of these needs and address them specifically to the church. The areas of need discussed below will serve as a brief summary, and at the same time will point to some conclusions for the ministering church.

Family isolation was discussed at length in Chapter 12. Inasmuch as isolation grows out of the absence of deeply meaningful relationships, the establishment of significant relatedness becomes the antidote for this ill of the family. An understanding of the deeper meanings of the church as a fellowship that undergirds and is concerned can be a powerful force in aiding families to escape their isolation. This concept of the church makes it the " family of God," with God as our Father and Jesus as our Elder Brother. Few have grasped the deeper meanings of the church to which the apostle Paul referred in Eph., ch. 5, when he depicted the relationship between Christ and the church as being analogous to relationships within the family. Since fears isolate people, those in the church must overcome isolating fears that prevent them from relating to one another as whole persons. Dietrich Bonhoeffer refers to some of these barriers between Christians in a passage from his book *Life Together:*

The final breakthrough to fellowship does not occur, because, though they have fellowship with one another as believers and as devout people, they do not have fellowship as the undevout, as sinners.[6]

Increasing family meaninglessness was seen to be a problem in Chapter 11. The church can address itself to this need perhaps more dramatically than can any other community institution. Meaninglessness arises when a person has lost his sense of ultimate purpose. A sense of purpose in the universe stands at the core of the Christian message. One of the chief problems, however, is that of being able to interpret this meaninglessness in terms and experiences intelligible to the man in the pew and at the same time present the gospel in terms that the listener finds understandable as an answer to this problem. Perhaps the minister would be aided in this task were he to look more closely within himself and realize that feelings of pointlessness occasionally plague him also.

The decline of religious bases of behavior was the problem to which Chapter 10 addressed itself. Even members of the church are acting on more and more secular values that often, though not necessarily, violate their religious faith. Religion, to be a potent force in the society, must influence behavior. Thus far, the rising tide of religious interest has seemingly failed to produce a corresponding elevation of ethical behavior. Serious discussions with businessmen, as well as with the laboring class, reveal that many of them feel that religion, at least as they know it, fails to come to grips with the cold realities of life out in the world. Religious ideals sound nice, they feel, but they are hardly practical. More interaction between the ministry and layman is needed in this area, perhaps in the form of down-to-earth discussions. Furthermore, it would be an educational experience in itself for each minister to spend at least a year living and working as a layman among those who do not know him as a minister. If such a "sabbatical" could be taken at the end of his first few years in the pastorate, it would give him an opportunity to test his preaching against life as his parishioners experience it. But perhaps this idea is not too practical.

The problems of the *unfulfilled woman* were discussed in Chapter 6. One aspect of this which is relevant to the church has to do with the need for more significant participation by women in the work of the church. It has been observed that when a group of men are planning something and come to

a point that evokes a " let the women do that," then one can
be sure this is some insignificant detail.[7] If women are already
searching for meaningful and significant activity, such experiences only aggravate the problem. Perhaps the church, more
than any other large organization of people, has been most
negligent about using the full potential and creative powers
of the female membership. A hopeful sign is seen in those
instances where women are occupying significant positions of
leadership in the church. One suspects that the popularity of
the women's auxiliaries in the church is partly traceable to
the fact that here, and only here, can they " run the show,"
as one thwarted wife observed. Some have long wondered
whether these organizations within the church were meeting
needs different from those for which they were specifically organized.

Increased leisure time presents a challenge and opportunity
to the church. With the prospects of the workweek becoming
shorter and shorter, more and more people will be looking to
their church for significant use of their leisure time. More lay
participation in the church will call for more effective pastor-
layman communication. Among other things, there could be
competition as to where the congregation is to look for its
major leadership. The following situation illustrates this problem. I was attending the annual state convention of a denomination in which a matter of controversial business came
to the floor involving several thousand dollars. A parade of
pastors argued at length the pros and cons of the issue. Finally,
one of the laymen, a businessman, gained the floor and in
such a manner as to give unmistakable evidence that his patience had been exhausted said: " Why don't you preachers
stick to your preaching. It's evident that you don't know anything about business matters! " The matter was summarily
dispatched.

Perhaps the minister will find the increased number of
capable and educated men and women who have time to devote to the church a threat to his leadership. At the same

time, it presents him with the opportunity to involve these people in activities of the church, thus relieving him for his own more distinctly pastoral functions.

The mobility of the family makes it difficult for the church to utilize the skills of its membership, as discussed in the paragraph above. First of all, there is the problem of discovering the abilities and interests of new families. As one pastor reported, " I didn't realize what a capable family they were and how much they had to offer the church until a few months before they were transferred." One highly educated woman reported being in her church four years without being asked to do one significant thing. However, during her first year in the P.T.A. she was appointed to one of their most responsible positions. Of course, one might argue that she should have put herself forth more at church, but the P.T.A. took time to discover her usable skills.

Mobility presents a second problem in the form of continuity of leadership. This is particularly acute in churches near large corporations that transfer their personnel often. A church may have ten of its families transferred at one time. Churches near military bases and in areas having resident tourists, such as Florida, confront similar problems.

Some of the needs of *people in the retirement years* were discussed in Chapter 9. The church is in a unique position to meet some of the spiritual and social-psychological needs of older people. It is easy to get lost in a modern church, whether one be young or old, or the church large or small. But if the church is large and one is old, it is doubly easy to get lost.

The undergirding fellowship of the church is best mediated through smaller groups within the church. It is not uncommon for a men's or women's group to be the one to carry on its shoulders some of the more lonely and isolated members. This sense of relatedness which was demonstrated recently in an older men's Sunday school class that I addressed was refreshing. Their singing, joking, praying, and studying all seemed to weld them together into a redemptive fellowship.

It is this kind of group experience which " heals the broken-hearted, and binds up their wounds " (Ps. 147:3) .

There are a group of family needs that challenge the church, depending upon the nature of the church membership and the community resources. To determine whether the church is growingly aware of certain needs, one need only look at what various churches are doing around them. In one city, a church offers a series of group sessions to engaged couples of the membership and calls in various specialists to lead the discussions. Another church has organized a group for the divorced people of its membership and of the community, recognizing that they have unique problems. Other churches have specialized ministries to the deaf and to the blind. Another church has regular meetings of the parents of the Sunday school children, in which parent-child relationships are discussed, and the responsibility of the home and parents in the religious development of the children is explored. Programs that minister to older people in the church are a part of the outreach of other churches.

Of course, such programs are not new in that certain churches across the nation have long found these and other programs to be effective ways of ministering to families in the church. The need is for more churches to broaden the scope of their outreach in making the gospel meaningful to the needs of the people within the " household of faith."

17

NEW HORIZONS FOR CHURCH AND FAMILY

ONE OF THE THINGS that makes life interesting and challenging is that there are always new horizons that beckon to us. The church, too, confronts these horizons. Because of this, its program and message need never become stale or irrelevant. The previous chapter underlined the necessity for the family and the church to work together and the necessity for the church to gear its program to the needs of its people. This chapter is concerned with three areas that are relevant to the needs of families in the church and that need developing. Although only three areas are mentioned, there are others that could be enumerated.

REEVALUATING OUR THEOLOGY OF FAMILY ROLES

The insights of modern behavioral sciences and the changes that have taken place in an industrialized society have created a need for reevaluating and reinterpreting our understanding of the roles of men and women. Jesus himself began this practice when he reinterpreted to first-century Christians their understanding of adultery. Previous to his time, adultery was interpreted by the Jews as being a sin committed mainly by a married woman. Men who become involved in extramarital affairs with another man's wife were guilty of violating another man's property rights.[1] Jesus attacks two of their misunderstandings in asserting, first, that adultery has its genesis in the heart, and secondly, that adultery also involves men, for "every one who looks at a woman lustfully has already committed adultery with her in *his* heart" (Matt. 5:28; emphasis mine).

"It's a man's world" run the words of an all-too-familiar saying. It would be almost trite to quote the phrase, were it not for the fact that in this mid-twentieth-century era it continues to be true in many ways. The truth is that it has been a man's world for countless centuries. This has permeated our attitudes, laws, and theology in so many ways that one can hardly think without using masculine concepts. At this point, a brief exploration shall be made of the impact of this masculine point of view on our theology.

One of the most challenging fields that need reevaluation and the application of insights from the behavioral sciences pertains to our understanding of the human situation from a feminine point of view. In an unusually provocative essay, Valerie Goldstein addresses herself to this problem.[2] Mrs. Goldstein asserts that since theology has been shaped by men in a masculine-dominated world, they have interpreted the human predicament in masculine concepts. This has led to a defining of the problems of both men and women on the basis of basically masculine conflicts. This reflection of a masculine theology is seen in the emphases of contemporary theology:

Its definition of the human situation in terms of anxiety, estrangement, and the conflict between necessity and freedom; its identification of sin with pride, will-to-power, exploitation, self-assertiveness, and the treatment of others as objects rather than persons; its conception of redemption as restoring to man what he fundamentally lacks (namely, sacrificial love, the I–Thou relationship, the primacy of the personal, and, ultimately, peace) — it is clear that such an analysis of man's dilemma was profoundly responsive and relevant to the concrete facts of modern man's existence.[3]

However, whereas this definition of the human situation is adequate for many men, it does not sufficiently describe the universal human situation, especially to the contemporary educated woman. Drawing from the various behavioral sciences, Mrs. Goldstein concludes that the point of view of women is basically different, deriving in part from the fact that nature has committed into her care the bearing of, and caring for, the young, and partly from the fact that society defines her role as pertaining to the home. Consequently, she feels that the temptations of women have a quality that can never be encompassed by masculine concepts such as " pride " and " will-to-power." The temptations of women are better described by terms such as: triviality, distractibility, and diffuseness, lack of an organizing center or focus, dependence on others for one's own self-definition, tolerance at the expense of standards of excellence, inability to respect the boundaries of privacy, sentimentality, gossipy sociability, and mistrust of reason.[4] Briefly, these are temptations which lead to a negation of the self or underdevelopment of the self.

If our society is being feminized, and many believe it is, then the feminine dilemma becomes important to men, and old understandings of sin may no longer ring true with men. The assembly line and automation leave men little room for self-discovery and self-expression (a current problem of women) and so the temptations of women described above become more and more real for men — tolerance at the expense of standards of excellence, lack of an organizing center, etc. Therefore, it becomes imperative that our understanding of the human situation be reevaluated in the light of the trends of the society, as sin manifests itself in new forms. Without this redefinition, our current masculine-oriented theology may be irrelevant to sin as experienced in our changing world.

In addition to reevaluating our theology in the light of feminine psychology, there also needs to be a reevaluation of our concepts of masculinity in the light of our new understandings of masculine psychology. In the sections of this book dealing with men, it has been noted that there is a new man emerging on the scene. This new man is more oriented toward the home and family and is giving expression to new and gentler emotions, the type of feelings formerly reserved for women. One of the chief values arising out of this new masculine psychology may very well be a more comfortable feeling with the New Testament picture of Jesus. For a long time many men seem to have been uncomfortable with the Biblical image of Jesus. In an era when men were supposed to be two-fisted, rugged, hairy-chested giants, the image of the gentle, compassionate, understanding, loving Jesus left men feeling most uncomfortable. Eagerly they searched the Gospels for a Jesus more in keeping with their image of a man. Because of this, the incident of Jesus throwing the money changers out of the Temple became much overworked. Ministers frequently felt called upon to affirm that being a Christian is no matter for women, children, and old men, and that Jesus was no "sissy." The very fact that such a defense was necessary is an indication that somehow the Jesus of the Bible did not seem to be thoroughly masculine. And the artists' portrayal of him with long hair did not help this situation.

What is being said here, however, is that the emerging new concept of a man so defines masculinity as to include both firmness and gentleness, decisiveness and forbearance. Perhaps what is being discovered is that, two thousand years ago, Jesus had achieved a fullness of manhood that modern men are just now beginning to grasp. This suggests that men who are *really* men are characterized by love, understanding, forgiveness, and gentleness, as well as by the more traditional qualities of firmness and decisiveness. Perhaps only real men are mature enough for such experiences.

A final area in which there needs to be a reevaluation has to do with integrating the Biblical understandings of husband-wife roles with those of the modern family. Attempts to apply *in toto* first-century, Middle Eastern, agrarian, patriarchal concepts of family roles to those of the twentieth century, American, industrial, urban, companionate family can only lead to frustrations, though it is sometimes tried. The admonition, " Wives, be subject to your husbands " (Eph. 5:22) is particularly difficult for modern couples to understand. The fact that husbands are exhorted to love their wives (Eph. 5:25) offers little comfort to the wife who sees in her subjection to her husband a renunciation, to some degree, of her own selfhood. Yet, if the Bible is still relevant to modern man's needs, and most of us believe it is, there must be an underlying truth applicable to the modern couple.

An excellent example of translating a Biblical teaching into language commensurate with modern family experience is to be found in Appendix II of Derrick Bailey's *The Mystery of Love and Marriage*. In it he deals with the problem of wifely subjection. What he says in essence is that Paul was not concerned with woman's social or legal status. Her subjection is, rather, of a nature of the subjection of equals to one another, a principle that finds expression in such everyday experiences as the employer and the employed, the ruler and the ruled.[5] Stated in other terms, this relationship might be thought of in terms of initiative and response. Pastors, counselors, and others working with people are aware of the fact that unless a woman has been hurt in unhappy experiences with her father or her husband, she usually wants to feel that her husband is looking after her, is, in a sense, " in charge " of the situation, and that she can look to him for strength. Of course, this in no way implies a renunciation of her own selfhood. This explanation does not answer all questions that one might have about husband-wife relationships as depicted in the Bible, but perhaps it does point the way to productive thinking.

EXPLORING THE NEW PASTOR-FAMILY ROLE

While the roles of men, women, and children have been undergoing transformation, so has the role of the pastor. At this point in history, pastors, along with others, are groping

to find their new role. When the pastor finds the most meaningful expression of his own role, then church-family leadership, as well as other areas crying for competent and mature
guidance, will become more stabilized. As one pastor remarked,
when confronted with the overwhelming family problems of
his parishioners: " I can't be too deeply concerned with their
problems right now. I've got too many fleas of my own to
scratch."

The traditional role of the pastor has made him a father
figure in the eyes of the congregation. This has been institu-
tionalized in the Roman Catholic Church, in which their
pastors are called " Father." As the role of the family father
has undergone change and confusion, the role of the pastor as
a father figure has also suffered. Pastors not only must examine the changing father role in relationship to their own
families, but their role to their parishioners as well. They have
a double-barreled role to change.

The old concept of a stern, patriarchal pastor, as is true of
such a father, is rapidly passing. Few of this tribe continue
to exist. The patriarchal pastors who remain communicate
the feeling of a firm and yet somewhat understanding father
and usually seem to " rule " their churches pretty well even
though the churches have a democratic structure. Somehow,
in a showdown, the weight of their personalities causes people
to vote as they desire. They may well have large congregations
of worshipful followers, for these people find a sense of security in their personalities.

Pastors are increasingly finding it difficult to follow the pattern of the patriarchal pastor. Young people are now imbued
with ideas of lay participation, democratic ideals, and the
equality of vocations. Many parishioners call their pastor by
his first name. One pastor of my acquaintance grew up in a
church that had long been dominated by the powerful personality of a much-loved patriarchal pastor. The church called
the younger man as pastor partly because of his association
with the older pastor whom they admired very much. How-

ever, when the new pastor began making unilateral decisions, as did his patriarchal mentor, the church rose up in arms, for they really did not want a patriarchal pastor for themselves.

If the pastor confronts difficulty in performing this traditional father-figure role in his relation to his people, then what other roles are available to him? Wayne Oates suggests that Protestant pastoral counselors will be more in touch with reality by de-emphasizing the father-figure dimension of Catholicism and psychoanalysis and exploring the distinctly Protestant understanding of the " brother-man relationship." [6] Indeed, in certain groups the title " Reverend " is considered distasteful, and the pastor is called " Brother." In this brother-man role the Protestant pastor differs radically from the Catholic priest, who operates by definition in the father role. The Protestant pastor is a fellow Christian with his people and acts as a father, Oates observes, in relation to his own children rather than in relation to his parishioners. He is of the opinion that the brother role offers more opportunity for growth on the part of parishioners or counselees than the father role, which connotes an over/under type of relationship. Also, if the role of the father is confused and is in a stage of transition, this would demand that the pastor work out only *one* such relationship — that to his own family. At least the " Father " priest has no wife and children crying for meaningful relationships.

The pastor confronts another problem in his relationships to families in the church, in that he is also related to them socially. This is both desirable and undesirable. It is desirable in that he is related to them as a fellow Christian. It is undesirable in that many of the pastor-parishioner conflicts that arise in a church can be traced partly to the fact that the pastor, in addition to having to tend to pastoral duties, also has to work out his social relationships with his people. Out of this arise hurt feelings, jealousies, and misunderstandings. The physician and lawyer can tend to the business of their clients without having to worry about insignificant trivia unrelated to the task at hand. In those instances in which the physician and lawyer also become personal friends with their clients, they run into similar problems as the pastor does, and their professional usefulness is frequently limited by the personal friendship.

Although the pastor continues to be a respected person in the community, many are concerned that his prestige has significantly declined. This was also discussed in the chapter concerned with the decline of religious values. The finest and most promising young men of the church at one time were challenged by the prospects of being a minister. Some denominational leaders are now distressed by the fact that in too many instances the young men entering ministerial training are those who have pronounced personality difficulties and/or seem to have hazy concepts of themselves as masculine persons. The ministry has also become, to some at least, an " easy living," with a certain status in the community. This is of concern to such educators as Ilion Jones who, in his book *The Pastor: The Man and His Ministry,* attempts to set forth the ministry as a vocation for men with a vision who are willing to be challenged to sacrifice for something in which they deeply believe, rather than spend time pitying themselves because of long hours and low pay.

One wonders what role seminary professors will play in helping the pastor to find a meaningful relationship to his parishioners. One might venture the guess that many men take as their pattern for future pastor-parishioner relationships that which they perceive in their relationship as a student to a favorite professor or to theological professors in general. If this student-professor relationship is heavily imbued with patriarchal overtones, one suspects that the student may attempt to work out this same awed relationship with the congregation when he becomes a pastor. However, not many democratic-minded congregations of today seem eager for such a relationship for themselves. The changing values of families who comprise the congregation demand that we search in new avenues for feelings of respect and importance, apart from these over/under relationships.

All this is to say that the nature and needs of the role of the modern pastor-man-father-husband must be integrated into a workable whole. The pastor has been caught, as have others, in the onrush of change. His own personal stability will bring stability to his ministry to others.

COURAGE TO EXPLORE NEW IDEAS

The church is often criticized for its conservatism. There are times when this criticism is justified. It is easy to let the *status quo* become the idol at whose feet we worship. But if the church is to be a dynamic force in the present and future, it cannot worship the past, nor fear the future. The first-century church did not reflect the ethics of the society, but, rather, seemed to set the pace. So impressive was the early Christians' faith that they were accused of turning the world upside down (Acts 17:6). Few churches today would be accused of turning the community, or anything in the community, upside down. And the necessity for war against misery, hate, greed, injustice, and suffering in our world has not become obsolete.

One of the challenges confronting the church concerns exploring new ideas with reference to ministering to families. A need for most church programs is for them to be more family- or person-centered rather than program-centered. Specific areas of need have been listed in the preceding chapter. What is meant here is that the total thrust, or religious philosophy, of a church's ministry, should have the needs of its families taken into consideration. Even here, one must recognize that the family is not to be worshiped, but the family must be led to worship and to conditions created so as to be conducive to worship. If this is done, it may mean reevaluating the denominational program in the light of local needs. Numbers of ministers privately express the opinion that the denominational program could be improved upon for meeting the needs in their local situation, but they continue to promote the program, apparently for the program's sake. Other church programs need to be changed entirely, they say, but it takes great courage to face one's colleagues were this to be done, because a daring pastor is often looked upon as a defector from the faith.

Those churches which dare to explore new ideas are often the churches with the most vibrant, alive program and enthusiastic, dedicated members. Among the churches that have dared to be different and to develop a meaningful religious philosophy of caring is the First Community Church of Columbus, Ohio. Under the leadership of the late Dr. Roy Burkhart, this church achieved national recognition because it attempted to minister to the needs of the people in the congregation in ways somewhat different from those of other churches. Another church that has departed from the conventional path is the Church of Our Saviour in Washington, D.C. This church has accepted into its fold many people who have been disenfranchised by the society and would be unacceptable in some other churches. They have developed an undergirding fellowship that ties each member to the other. Their procedure, among other things, includes financial aid, help in time of illness, and a sense of concern for those who find life bearing down on them rather heavily. All this stems from a profound spiritual atmosphere. The surprising thing about these two " different " churches is that in a very real sense they are not different at all; they have simply rediscovered the truth by which early Christians lived, which basically involves koinōnia, or a profound sense of fellowship that includes a sense of responsibility for, and relatedness to, fellow believers.

Churches need to have the courage to explore new ideas even though these may not attract the masses of people. Pastors frequently deplore the emphasis on numbers, but then continue to work feverishly to involve more and more people in the church's program. What churches really need is people with greater dedication, rather than great numbers. Most movements are not accomplished by the masses but by a few deeply dedicated people. One need look no farther than the history of Christianity to see this truth. This is also the history of communism.

Modern churches might look anew at Jesus' parable of the lost sheep. Churches that are primarily concerned with the masses, the respectable, the majority, are likely to lose their sense of mission. Although one must not forget the ninety and nine sheep, the thing that often provides a sense of purpose and direction for the ninety and nine is concern over the one that is lost. The church is probably never more fully the church than when it unites to minister to some "lost sheep," possibly some minority group. There are these needy minority groups in almost every community. The deaf, blind, crippled, and aging are among these. The church that begins a ministry to, say, the deaf will find the whole membership benefiting from the service. It is an inspiring experience to see these people "singing" a hymn with their hands while an interpreter leads them, as the rest of the congregation worship with their voices. The tragically twisted bodies of cerebral-palsied children can make people uncomfortable, but a worship service takes on new meaning as one sits in a congregation with these children from a special home and knows that these too are God's children and that one of the highlights of their lonely week is the Sunday trip to church.

The increasing number of mothers who do, or must, work offers a fertile field for churches with a vision. One of the most shameful wastes of space in the community is the church's expensive educational building that stands empty all week except for one or two hours Sunday and a few scattered meetings during the week. Some churches are making use of the space as day nurseries for working mothers. One of the major problems of women who work, many of whom are widowed or divorced and have no other choice, is providing adequate care for their children during the day at a price they can afford. These too are "lost sheep."

People are both challenged and threatened by something new. Churches that rise to the needs of their people to meet them, whether by conventional or unconventional methods, will discover the challenge of a revitalized faith. If the church is to capture the imagination of the people and set the pace in standards of living and in the caliber of its love, it must have the courage to remain loyal to the old ways that have proven their validity, as well as exploring new ways to meet new needs.

Long ago the Master said, "I am come that they may have life and that they may have it more abundantly" (John 10:10). The family, with its pronounced areas of conflicts and growing potential for strength, offers a challenge to the church not extended to any other organization in the community to make this life more abundant.

NOTES

Chapter 2. INDUSTRIAL PROGRESS AND FAMILY CHANGE

1. William F. Ogburn and M. F. Nimkoff, *Technology and the Changing Family* (Houghton Mifflin Company, 1955), p. 21.
2. *Ibid.*, p. iii.
3. *Ibid.*, p. 7.
4. Paul W. Alexander, " Our Legal Horror — Divorce," article in *Ladies' Home Journal,* reprinted in *Current Approaches to Delinquency,* ed. by Marjorie Bell (1949 yearbook of the National Probation & Parole Association, 1950), p. 141.
5. Roland Bainton, *What Christianity Says About Sex, Love and Marriage* (Reflection Book, Association Press, 1957), pp. 37–39.
6. Ogburn and Nimkoff, *op. cit.,* p. 114.
7. *Ibid.,* p. iii.
8. *Ibid.,* p. 122.
9. *Ibid.,* p. 10.

Chapter 3. SHIFTING ROLES OF THE FAMILY

1. Ernest Groves, *Social Problems of the Family* (J. B. Lippincott Company, 1927), pp. 1–5, 55–65.
2. William F. Ogburn, " Social Heritage and the Family," *Family Life Today,* ed. by M. E. Rich (Houghton Mifflin Company, 1928), p. 31.
3. M. F. Nimkoff, *The Family* (Houghton Mifflin Company, 1934), pp. 47–97.
4. Ernest Burgess and Harvey Locke, *The Family: From Institution to Companionship* (American Book Company, 1945), pp. 501–511.
5. Nathan Ackerman, *The Psychodynamics of Family Life: Diagnosis and Treatment of Family Relationships* (Basic Books, Inc., Publishers, 1958), p. 19.
6. Burgess and Locke, *op. cit.,* p. 502.

7. Enrico Quarantelli, " A Note on the Protective Function of the Family in Disasters," *Marriage and Family Living*, 22:263-264 (August, 1960) .
8. Burgess and Locke, *op. cit.* (1953 edition) , pp. 510-511.
9. Howard Halpern, " Alienation from Parenthood in the Kibbutz and America," *Marriage and Family Living*, 24:42-45 (February, 1962) .
10. Ackerman, *op. cit.*, p. 339.

Chapter 4.   THE INFLUENCE OF PROTESTANTISM ON THE FAMILY

1. Roy W. Fairchild and John C. Wynn, *Families in the Church: A Protestant Survey* (Association Press, 1961) , p. 93.
2. David Soper, *Epistle to the Skeptics* (Association Press, 1956) .
3. Fairchild and Wynn, *op. cit.*, p. 93.
4. Paul Tillich, *The Courage to Be* (Yale University Press, 1952) , p. 114.
5. William Graham Cole, *Sex in Christianity and Psychoanalysis* (Oxford University Press, Inc., 1955) , p. 57.
6. Roland Bainton, *What Christianity Says About Sex, Love and Marriage* (Reflection Book, Association Press, 1957) , p. 43.
7. *Ibid.*, p. 30.
8. Roland Bainton, *Here I Stand* (Abingdon Press, 1950) , p. 286.
9. Cole, *op. cit.*, p. 37.
10. *Ibid.*, p. 106.
11. Bainton, *What Christianity Says About Sex, Love and Marriage*, p. 75.
12. Fairchild and Wynn, *op. cit.*, p. 94.
13. *Ibid.*, p. 102.
14. Cole, *op. cit.*, pp. 109-110.
15. John Dillenberger and Claude Welch, *Protestant Christianity Interpreted Through Its Development* (Charles Scribner's Sons, 1954) , p. 325.
16. Cole, *op. cit.*, p. 105.
17. Fairchild and Wynn, *op. cit.*, p. 19.
18. Cole, *op. cit.*, p. 119.
19. Bainton, *Here I Stand*, p. 384.

Chapter 5.   DEMASCULINIZED MEN

1. William Kenkel, *The Family in Perspective* (Appleton-Century-Crofts, 1960) , p. 67.
2. Carle Zimmerman, *Family and Civilization* (Harper & Brothers, 1947) , p. 338.
3. David and Vera Mace, *Marriage: East and West* (Doubleday & Company, Inc., 1960) , p. 49.
4. *Ibid.*, p. 50.
5. O. Spurgeon English, " Three Common Sexual Problems: Masturbation, Homosexuality, and Impotence and Frigidity," *Man and Wife*, ed. by Emily Mudd and Aaron Krich (W. W. Norton & Company, Inc., 1957) , p. 196.

6. Harry F. Tashman, *The Marriage Bed* (University Publishers, Inc., 1959), p. 101.

7. Howard Clinebell, *Understanding and Counseling the Alcoholic* (Abingdon Press, 1956), p. 50.

8. Robert O. Blood and D. M. Wolfe, *Husbands and Wives: The Dynamics of Married Living* (The Free Press of Glencoe, 1960), pp. 12–13.

9. Ralph Linton, *The Study of Man* (Appleton-Century-Crofts, Inc., 1936), p. 117.

10. Margaret Mead, *Male and Female* (Mentor Book, New American Library of World Literature, Inc., 1955), p. 125.

11. Valerie Goldstein, "The Human Situation: A Feminine Viewpoint," *The Nature of Man in Theological and Psychological Perspective*, ed. by Simon Doniger (Harper & Brothers, 1962), p. 158.

12. *Ibid.*, pp. 157–158.

13. *Ibid.*, p. 158.

14. *Ibid.*, p. 159.

15. Helen M. Hacker, "The New Burdens of Masculinity," *Marriage and Family Living*, 19:227–233 (August, 1957).

16. Florence Kluckhohn, "The American Family and the Feminine Role," *Human Relations*, Vol. I, ed. by Hugh Cabot and Joseph Kahl (Harvard University Press, 1953), p. 249.

17. D. W. Brogan, *American Themes* (Harper & Brothers, 1947), p. 37.

18. Daniel Brown, "Masculinity-Femininity Development in Children," *Journal of Consulting Psychology*, 21:197–202 (June, 1957).

19. Albert Ellis, "Marriage Counseling with Demasculinizing Wives and Demasculinized Husbands," *Marriage and Family Living*, 22:13–21 (February, 1960).

20. Carl Rogers, *On Becoming a Person* (Houghton Mifflin Company, 1961), pp. 31–38.

Chapter 6. UNFULFILLED WOMEN

1. Anne Morrow Lindbergh, *Gift from the Sea* (Signet Book, New American Library of World Literature, Inc., 1957).

2. Valerie Goldstein, "The Human Situation: A Feminine Viewpoint," *The Nature of Man in Theological and Psychological Perspective*, ed. by Simon Doniger (Harper & Brothers, 1962).

3. Paul Morentz, "The Image of the Seminary Wife," *Pastoral Psychology*, 12:51 (December, 1961).

4. Paul Landis, *Making the Most of Marriage* (Appleton-Century-Crofts, Inc., 1953), p. 57.

5. Edward Ellis and George Allen, *The Traitor Within* (Doubleday & Company, Inc., 1961), p. 126.

6. Robert Coughlan, "Changing Roles in Modern Marriage," *Life*, 41:109 (December 24, 1956).

7. Personal Conference with Dr. Kermit Phelps, who is Chief of Psychology Service, V.A. Hospital, Kansas City, Missouri.

8. Florence Kluckhohn, "The American Family and the Feminine

Role," *Human Relations*, Vol. I, ed. by Hugh Cabot and Joseph Kahl (Harvard University Press, 1953) , p. 268.

9. Florence Kluckhohn, "What's Wrong with the American Family? " *Journal of Social Hygiene*, 36:232 (June, 1950) .

10. Nelson Foote, " Changes in American Marriage Patterns," *Eugenics Quarterly*, 1:254 (December, 1954) .

11. Margaret Mead, in a television discussion of the " trapped housewife." Quoted by George Lefferts, *Special for Women* (Avon Book Division, The Hearst Corporation, 1960, 1961) , p. 110.

12. *Ibid.*, p. 49.

13. George Belane, " Faculty Wives," *Harper's Magazine*, 168:462 (March, 1934) .

14. Kluckhohn, " The American Family and the Feminine Role," *loc. cit.*, p. 278.

15. Ray Baber, *Marriage and Family* (McGraw-Hill Book Company, Inc., 1953) , p. 379.

16. David Mace, " The Employed Mother in the U.S.S.R.," *Marriage and Family Living*, 23:330–333 (November, 1961) .

17. Kluckhohn, " The American Family and the Feminine Role," *loc. cit.*, p. 280.

18. Lamar Empey, " Role Expectations of Young Women Regarding Marriage and a Career," *Marriage and Family Living*, 20:153 (May, 1958) .

19. Nelson Foote, *loc. cit.*, p. 258.

20. Emil Brunner, *The Divine Imperative*, tr. by Olive Wyon (The Westminster Press, 1947) , p. 376.

Chapter 7. ANXIOUS PARENTS

1. Nathan Ackerman, *The Psychodynamics of Family Life* (Basic Books, Inc., Publishers, 1958) , p. 113.

2. Anneliese Korner, " The Parent Takes the Blame," *Social Casework*, 42:339–342 (July, 1961) .

3. George Stevenson and Harry Milt, *Master Your Tensions and Enjoy Living Again* (Prentice-Hall, Inc., 1959) , p. 5.

4. William H. Sheldon is the author of several books, but his *Varieties of Human Physique* (1940) and *Varieties of Temperament* (1942) , both published by Harper & Brothers, set forth some of his basic concepts.

5. John Watson, *The Psychological Care of Infant and Child.* (W. W. Norton & Company, Inc., 1928) .

6. Korner, *loc. cit.*

7. Nelson Foote, " Changes in American Marriage Patterns," *Eugenics Quarterly*, 1:257 (December, 1954) .

Chapter 8. ACCELERATED LIVING

1. Samuel Grafton, " Why Teen-Age Marriages Are Falling Apart," *McCall's*, 87:89 (November, 1959) .

2. Cited by Burk Uzzle, "Boys and Girls: Too Old Too Soon," *Life,* 53:62 (August 10, 1962).
3. Kansas City (Missouri) *Times,* January 4, 1962.
4. Uzzle, *loc. cit.*
5. *Ibid.,* p. 63.
6. Michel Silva, "What Some Parents Did to Clamp Down," *Life,* 53:69 (August 10, 1962).
7. David Mace, "Radical Proposal: Let's Abolish Dating Under Fifteen," *McCall's,* 88:96–97 ff. (August, 1961).

Chapter 9. LONGER YEARS OF RETIREMENT

1. George Lawton, *Aging Successfully* (Columbia University Press, 1946), p. 119.
2. Louis Linn and Leo Schwarz, *Psychiatry and Religious Experience* (Random House, Inc., 1958), p. 212.
3. Paul Maves and J. Lennart Cedarleaf, *Older People and the Church* (Abingdon-Cokesbury Press, 1949), p. 136.
4. Max Lerner, *America as a Civilization* (Simon and Schuster, Inc., 1957), p. 613.
5. Elaine Cumming and William Henry, *Growing Old* (Basic Books, Inc., Publishers, 1961).
6. *Ibid.,* pp. 147–149.
7. Lawton, *op. cit.,* p. 65.
8. *Ibid.,* p. 107.
9. *Basic Works of Cicero,* ed. by Moses Hadas (Modern Library, Random House, Inc., 1951), p. 128.
10. Maves and Cedarleaf, *op. cit.,* p. 54.
11. Robert Gray and David Moberg, *The Church and the Older Person* (Wm. B. Eerdmans Publishing Company, 1962), pp. 122–125.
12. *Ibid.,* p. 60.
13. *Ibid.,* p. 59.
14. Paddy Chayefsky, *Television Plays* (Simon and Schuster, Inc., 1955), p. 156.
15. Gray and Moberg, *op. cit.,* pp. 137–144.
16. Lawton, *op. cit.,* p. 171.

Chapter 10. THE DECLINE OF RELIGIOUS BASES OF BEHAVIOR

1. Religious News Service dispatch, Wichita (Kansas) *Light* (All-Church Press, Publisher), November 30, 1962.
2. Cited by Lyle M. Spencer, "The Changing Face of Children's Heroes," *The PTA Magazine,* 57:9 (November, 1962).
3. Martin E. Marty, *The New Shape of American Religion* (Harper & Brothers, 1959), p. 15.
4. Benson Y. Landis, ed., *Yearbook of American Churches,* edition for 1963 (Office of Publication and Distribution, National Council of the Churches of Christ in the U.S.A.), pp. 248, 274.

5. Marty, *op. cit.*, p. 37.

6. *Ibid.*, pp. 37–39.

7. Norman Bell and Ezra Vogel, " Toward a Framework for Functional Analysis of Family Behavior," *A Modern Introduction to the Family*, ed. by Norman Bell and Ezra Vogel (The Free Press of Glencoe, 1960), p. 18.

8. Roy W. Fairchild and John C. Wynn, *Families in the Church: A Protestant Survey* (Association Press, 1961), pp. 34–35.

9. Cited by Negley Teeters and John Reineman, *The Challenge of Delinquency* (Prentice-Hall, Inc., 1950), p. 163.

10. Hector J. Ritey, *The Human Kingdom* (University Publishers, Inc., 1962).

Chapter 11.   INCREASING FAMILY MEANINGLESSNESS

1. Viktor Frankl, *From Death-Camp to Existentialism: A Psychiatrist's Path to a New Therapy* (Beacon Press, Inc., 1959).

2. *Ibid.*, p. 103.

3. A. J. Ungersma, *The Search for Meaning: A New Approach in Psychotherapy and Pastoral Psychology* (The Westminster Press, 1961).

4. Viktor Frankl, " Psychiatry and Man's Quest for Meaning," *Journal of Religion and Mental Health*, 1:93 (January, 1962).

5. Émile Cailliet, *The Recovery of Purpose* (Harper & Brothers, 1959).

6. *Ibid.*, p. 17.

7. *Ibid.*, p. 20.

8. *Ibid.*

9. *Ibid.*, pp. 91–92.

10. Sigmund Freud, *Civilization and Its Discontents*, tr. by Joan Riviere (Hogarth Press, Ltd., London, 1930), p. 26.

11. W. T. Stace, " Man Against Darkness," *Atlantic*, 182:54 (September, 1948).

12. Howard Halpern, " Alienation from Parenthood in the Kibbutz and America," *Marriage and Family Living*, 24:42–45 (February, 1962).

13. Carl Jung, *Modern Man in Search of a Soul*, tr. by W. S. Dell and Cary Baynes (Harcourt, Brace and World, Inc., 1933), p. 264.

14. Frankl, " Psychiatry and Man's Quest for Meaning," *loc. cit.*, p. 94.

15. Paul Tillich, *The Courage to Be* (Yale University Press, 1952), p. 47.

16. Vance Packard, *The Waste Makers* (David McKay Company, Inc., 1960), p. 326.

Chapter 12.   FAMILY ISOLATION

1. Paul Tournier, *Escape from Loneliness*, tr. by John S. Gilmour (The Westminster Press, 1962).

2. Henry Guntrip, *Psychotherapy and Religion* (Harper & Brothers, 1957), pp. 98–103.

3. Gibson Winter, *Love and Conflict* (Doubleday & Company, Inc., 1958).

4. *Ibid.*, pp. 182–183.

5. Tournier, *op. cit.*, p. 125.

6. Theodor Reik, *Listening with the Third Ear: The Inner Experience of a Psychoanalyst* (Farrar, Straus & Young, Inc., 1948).

7. Taylor Caldwell, *The Listener* (Bantam Books, Inc., 1962), p. vii.

Chapter 13. THE STRENGTHENED ROLES OF FAMILY MEMBERS

1. A. H. Maslow, "Love in Healthy People," *The Meaning of Love*, ed. by Ashley Montagu (The Julian Press, Inc., 1953), p. 91.

2. Carle Zimmerman and Lucius Cervantes, *Successful American Families* (Pageant Press, 1960), p. 205.

3. Florence Kluckhohn, "What's Wrong with the American Family?" *Journal of Social Hygiene*, 36:232 (June, 1950).

4. Nelson Foote, "Changes in American Marriage Patterns," *Eugenics Quarterly*, 1:257 (December, 1954).

5. J. M. Mogey, "A Century of Declining Paternal Authority," *Marriage and Family Living*, 19:238 (August, 1957).

6. Jerome and Julia Rainer, "Tenderness: A New Style in Masculinity," *Coronet*, 47:172–175 (February, 1960), excerpt from *Sexual Pleasure in Marriage* (Julian Messner, Inc., Publishers, 1959).

7. Irene Josselyn, "Psychology of Fatherliness," *Smith College Studies in Social Work*, 26:1–13 (February, 1956).

8. Cited by Elisabeth Dodd, "Don't Pity Your Pastor's Wife," *Presbyterian Life*, 11:16–18 (January 11, 1958).

9. Nathan Ackerman, *The Psychodynamics of Family Life* (Basic Books, Inc., Publishers, 1958), p. 179.

10. Wallace Jamie, "Women: Our Other Great Resource," *Journal of College Placement*, 18:15 (December, 1957).

11. David and Vera Mace, *Marriage: East and West* (Doubleday & Company, Inc., 1960), p. 71.

12. William F. Ogburn and M. F. Nimkoff, *Technology and the Changing Family* (Houghton Mifflin Company, 1955), p. 185.

13. Esther Rauschenbush, "Second Chance: New Education for Women," *Harper's Magazine*, 225:147–151 (October, 1962).

14. Associated Press News release, Kansas City (Missouri) *Times*, June 5, 1962.

15. Ogburn and Nimkoff, *op. cit.*, p. 11.

16. Lamar Empey, "Role Expectations of Young Women Regarding Marriage and a Career," *Marriage and Family Living*, 20:152 (May, 1958).

17. Max Lerner, *America as a Civilization* (Simon and Schuster, Inc., 1957), p. 608.

18. Foote, *loc. cit.*, p. 258.

19. Lerner, *op. cit.*, p. 611.

20. Kenneth Scott Latourette, *A History of Christianity* (Harper & Brothers, 1953), pp. 258–259.

21. Madeleine Barot, "Considerations on the Need for a Theology of the Place of Women in the Church," *The Ecumenical Review*, 7:151–160 (January, 1955).

22. Gibson Winter, *Love and Conflict* (Doubleday & Company, Inc., 1958) , p. 39.

23. Katherine Oettinger, "Children in a Changing World," *Marriage and Family Living,* 20:238 (August, 1958) .

24. Ogburn and Nimkoff, *op. cit.,* p. 196.

25. Paul Popenoe and C. E. Phillips, "Heredity and Counseling," *Family Life,* 22:1–4 (October, 1962) .

26. Joan Lasko, "Parent-Child Relationships: Report from the Fels Research Institute," *American Journal of Orthopsychiatry,* 22:301 (April, 1952) .

Chapter 14. STRENGTHENED MARRIAGE CONCEPTS

1. Ernest Burgess and Harvey Locke, *The Family: From Institution to Companionship* (American Book Company, 1945) , p. vii.

2. Robert O. Blood and D. M. Wolfe, *Husbands and Wives: The Dynamics of Married Living* (The Free Press of Glencoe, 1960) , p. 191.

3. *Ibid.,* pp. 194–195.

4. Henlee Barnette, *Introducing Christian Ethics* (Broadman Press, 1961) , pp. 111–112.

5. William Graham Cole, *Sex in Christianity and Psychoanalysis* (Oxford University Press, Inc., 1955) , pp. 119–120.

6. Max Lerner, *America as a Civilization* (Simon and Schuster, Inc., 1957) , p. 595.

7. Alfred Kinsey, *et al.,* *Sexual Behavior in the Human Female* (W. B. Saunders Company, 1953) , p. 11.

8. Ernest Burgess, "The Wise Choice of a Mate," *Successful Marriage,* ed. by Morris Fishbein and Ernest Burgess (Doubleday & Company, Inc., 1947) , p. 19.

9. Paul Popenoe, "Can the Family Have Two Heads?" *Sociology and Social Research,* 18:12–17 (September–October, 1933) .

10. Helen Ingersoll, "A Study of the Transmission of Authority Patterns in the Family," *Genetic Psychology Monographs,* 38:292 (1948) .

11. Thomas Knight, "In Defense of Romance," *Marriage and Family Living,* 21:107–110 (May, 1959) .

12. Lerner, *op. cit.,* p. 583.

13. James Peterson, *Education for Marriage* (Charles Scribner's Sons, 1956) , p. 13.

14. Charles Hobart, "Disillusionment in Marriage and Romanticism," *Marriage and Family Living,* 20:156–162 (May, 1958) .

15. Henry Bowman, "How Can You Tell if It Is Love?" Fishbein and Morris, eds., *op. cit.,* p. 7.

16. Willard Waller, *The Family: A Dynamic Interpretation* (The Cordon Company, 1938) , p. 200.

17. Personal conference with Dr. O. J. Hodges, director of the Ozark Christian Counseling Service, Springfield, Missouri.

18. Waller, *op. cit.,* p. 353.

19. Willard Waller, *The Family: A Dynamic Interpretation,* revised by

Reuben Hill (The Dreyden Press, Inc., 1951), p. 362.

20. Søren Kierkegaard, "The Aesthetic Validity of Marriage," *A Kierkegaard Anthology*, ed. by Robert Bretall (Princeton University Press, 1947), p. 91.

21. Theodor Reik, *A Psychologist Looks at Love* (Farrar & Rinehart, Inc., 1944), p. 299.

Chapter 15. STRENGTH THROUGH LEISURE AND FLEXIBILITY

1. Max Kaplan, *Leisure in America: A Social Inquiry* (John Wiley & Son, Inc., 1960), p. 151.

2. *Ibid.*

3. *Home and Highway*, Spring, 1962, p. 12.

4. Sebastian de Grazia, *Of Time, Work and Leisure* (Twentieth Century Fund, 1962).

5. Florence Kluckhohn, "The American Family and the Feminine Role," *Human Relations*, Vol. I, ed. by Hugh Cabot and Joseph Kahl (Harvard University Press, 1953), p. 277.

6. *Ibid.*

7. Karl Menninger, *Love Against Hate* (Harcourt, Brace and Company, 1942), p. 185.

8. Viktor Frankl, "Psychiatry and Man's Quest for Meaning," *Journal of Religion and Mental Health*, 1:93–103 (January, 1962).

9. Donald Super, "Education and the Nature of Occupations and Careers," *Teachers College Record*, 58:301–309 (March, 1957).

10. "The Do-It-Yourself Market," *Mass Leisure*, ed. by Eric Larrabee and Rolf Meyerson (The Free Press of Glencoe, 1958), p. 275.

11. *Ibid.*, p. 278.

12. Boris Blair, "Your Happiness Is in Your Hands," *Reader's Digest*, 80:129 (June, 1962).

13. Menninger, *op. cit.*, pp. 186–187.

14. *Newsweek*, 59:96 (June 4, 1962).

15. Sidney Goldstein, *Patterns of Mobility 1910–1950* (University of Pennsylvania Press, 1958), p. 235.

16. William Whyte, Jr., "The Corporation and the Wife," *Fortune*, 44:152 (November, 1951).

17. Nelson Foote, "Changes in American Marriage Patterns," *Eugenics Quarterly*, 1:256 (December, 1954).

18. William Whyte, Jr., *The Organization Man* (Anchor Book, Doubleday & Company, Inc., 1957), pp. 319–320.

Chapter 16. THE CHURCH AND FAMILY NEEDS

1. Ernest Groves, *Christianity and the Family* (The Macmillan Company, 1942), pp. 3–21.

2. *Ibid.*, p. 5.

3. John Charles Wynn, *Pastoral Ministry to Families* (The Westminster Press, 1957), p. 19.

4. *Ibid.*, p. 21.
5. *Ibid.*, p. 23.
6. Dietrich Bonhoeffer, *Life Together* (Harper & Brothers, 1954), p. 110.
7. Florence Kluckhohn, " The American Family and the Feminine Role," *Human Relations*, Vol. I, ed. by Hugh Cabot and Joseph Kahl (Harvard University Press, 1953), p. 273.

Chapter 17. New Horizons for Church and Family

1. David Mace, *Hebrew Marriage* (The Epworth Press, Publishers, London, 1953), p. 227.
2. Valerie Goldstein, " The Human Situation: A Feminine Viewpoint," *The Nature of Man in Theological and Psychological Perspective*, ed. by Simon Doniger (Harper & Brothers, 1962), pp. 151–170.
3. *Ibid.*, p. 163.
4. *Ibid.*, p. 165.
5. Derrick S. Bailey, *The Mystery of Love and Marriage* (Harper & Brothers, 1952), pp. 129–130.
6. Wayne E. Oates, *Protestant Pastoral Counseling* (The Westminster Press, 1962), pp. 139–144.